"It Mattered to Me"

A tribute to the life and lessons of
William Beeber, R.Ph.

Jeffrey M. Stamps, R.Ph.

TABLE OF CONTENTS

Preface

    This book is dedicated to the life of William Beeber, R.Ph. In addition to being a devoted husband, loving father, and successful entrepreneur, Mr. Beeber was, to my everlasting good fortune, my business mentor. Mr. Beeber and I crossed paths when I was just an impressionable young pharmacy student, and he made a broad and lasting impact on both my career and my personal life.

    Everyone who encountered Mr. Beeber knew that his driving passion was the pharmacy profession, and he was dedicated to the task of teaching other pharmacists about all aspects of the business. I am indebted to him for the many ways he invested himself in me. Over the course of my 30-year pharmacy career, I frequently talked about Mr. Beeber, and I tried to teach others the principles he ingrained in me. Many have encouraged me to write down these "Mr. Beeber lessons," so this book is my attempt to honor Mr. Beeber by encapsulating his business philosophy and code of conduct. Putting these stories in writing has given me an opportunity to appreciate all over again the incomparable, colorful character that was William Beeber.

    This book is for you, Mr. B.!! I remain immensely appreciative for the many lessons you passed along to me.

CHAPTER 1

"Don't be late!"

It was May 1982, and I was just finishing my first year of the undergraduate professional pharmacy program at the University of Cincinnati. At that time, Ohio required each pharmacy student to complete coursework and serve as a pharmacist intern for a minimum of 1,500 hours before sitting for the licensure examination. To this point, I had not completed any hours toward my 1,500-hour requirement, so I was a bit behind, to say the least. It was imperative that I intern during the coming summer, even though I expected to earn far less than the $8.00 per hour I was paid for overnight shifts at the printing factory where my father was a foreman. Like most college students at the time, it took everything I could make or borrow, plus a significant contribution on the part of my parents, to cover the costs of my education. Having resigned myself to the lower pay, it was time to look for a position as a pharmacist intern.

I had been told by a classmate that a pharmacy not too far from my parents' home might be looking for an intern. So on June 1, 1982, for no real reason other than its proximity to my parents' residence, I walked into Beeber Pharmacy on Main Street in Trotwood, Ohio. Summoning all the courage an introvert needs for such a situation, I asked the person at the counter if I could fill out an application. She was somewhat aloof in her reply and quickly went into the back room. A few minutes later, she returned and said, "The owner of the pharmacy is here. Do you have time to interview right now?" I replied,

"Of course I do," and sat down quickly so as not to interfere with the business of the pharmacy, which I could see was quite robust.

Within a few minutes a friendly, middle-aged man bounded around the corner, reaching out his hand and saying enthusiastically, "Good afternoon! My name is Bill Beeber, and I am the owner of the pharmacy." After I introduced myself and indicated my interest in applying for a pharmacist intern position, he invited me into the back room, where his next statement caught me a bit off guard: "Jeff, are you willing to work for minimum wage, and can you start tomorrow at 6:00 a.m. sharp, and I mean sharp? Don't be late!" It wasn't exactly the probing and thorough interview I was expecting, but I quickly answered 'yes' to both questions so as to leave no doubt about my interest. Mr. Beeber shook my hand when I accepted his offer, saying he would see me in the morning. As he prepared to pass me along to his office manager, something inside of me made me ask, "What are we going to be doing at 6:00 in the morning? Is there something in particular I need to be prepared for?" He looked at me, smiled, and in a very engaging tone, stated, "Yes, Jeff, we are going to a nursing home tomorrow. I am sure it will be a new experience for you. Please dress professionally, which means a tie and a white lab coat." With that, Mr. Beeber introduced me to his office manager so I could fill out the necessary forms, and then he went on his way.

I left Beeber Pharmacy that day walking on air. I had a job as a pharmacy intern and was on my way to becoming a pharmacist someday! Little did I know as I walked out of the pharmacy that my 'interview' would be, in essence, the only interview I would have in what would become a 30-year career in long-term care pharmacy, ending with my role as executive vice president and president of operations of the nation's largest provider of such services. Without a doubt, William Beeber would become the most influential person ever to cross my professional path, and with the exception of close family members, would have the greatest impact on my personal development as well.

I barely slept the night of June 1, being both eager and nervous about starting my new job the next day. I woke up early, concerned about oversleeping, and dressed as I had been instructed. I arrived at the pharmacy about 5:45, and Mr. Beeber was there waiting for me. He offered me a cheerful 'good morning,' ushered me into his Volvo station wagon (a car he drove as his vehicle of choice throughout our years together), and off we went. Today was to be the first of many visits to nursing homes. Beeber Pharmacy, in addition to being a retail pharmacy, also did considerable business as a long-term care (LTC) pharmacy. In this capacity, Mr. Beeber and his staff pharmacists contracted with long-term care facilities to provide on-site dispensing of medications and to consult with staff members on matters related to their patients' pharmaceutical needs.

This particular visit was to a facility in Springfield, Ohio, to "set them up on our institutional service." Since this was a new account, our job was to gather the necessary documents so we could enter the resident information into the computer back at the pharmacy. Once we began working around 7:30, it became clear it would be a long day, simply by virtue of the amount of information we needed to gather. I sat beside Mr. Beeber, working diligently throughout the morning and well past the lunch hour. Sometime around 2:00 p.m., my stomach began growling loudly. Mr. Beeber looked up, almost with a sly grin on his face and said, "Jeff, you have to work hard as a pharmacist if you want to succeed. We don't take lunch hours, so hopefully next time you will come better prepared." I didn't say a word, but just kept my head down and continued working. I was thankful when we finally completed our work around 5:30 p.m. On the way home, Mr. Beeber never offered to stop for anything to eat, as he had dinner plans and wanted to get home. As he dropped me off at the pharmacy, he looked at me and said, "Never underestimate the importance of grunt work in a pharmacy." And with that, my career with Mr. Beeber was off to an interesting start!

CHAPTER 2

Medicine or Pharmacy?

From the time I was very young, I had an interest in medicine, such that when I entered college, I intended to become a physician, not a pharmacist. I spent my first two years of college at the University of South Carolina at Spartanburg (now called USC Upstate), where I played basketball. My first year was a bit shaky from a grades perspective, but during the second year, I was able to make very high marks. After my second year, I returned home to Dayton for a visit and met someone who was attending the University of Cincinnati College of Pharmacy. Our discussion about the pharmacy program intrigued me for two reasons. First, I learned that the pharmacy program was highly specialized, and upon completion, would provide graduates with extensive knowledge about all aspects of pharmaceutical care. Second, it offered a great way to get into medical school. It also didn't hurt that pharmacists were well-paid professionals, and as with most college students, I was tired of being broke. As I saw it, pharmacy school offered an appealing way to get a meaningful degree that would also equip me to get a good part-time job while I was in medical school.

I applied to the University of Cincinnati's pharmacy school and was admitted for the 1981 fall term. I transferred from South Carolina and was immediately impressed with the caliber of the pharmacy program and its instructors. The program was a good fit for me, and I flourished academically. It was after my first year of pharmacy school that I interned at Beeber Pharmacy.

Mr. Beeber recognized that I had a keen interest in the clinical side of pharmacy, so he focused the training he gave me accordingly. Mr. Beeber was not your typical preceptor (the person at the internship site managing the educational experience of the student), in that he actually took time to work with me. During my internship at Beeber, I constantly heard stories from my fellow students about preceptors who simply "put them to work" in their pharmacy and did nothing to further the students' education. Mr. Beeber was just the opposite. He loved nothing better than to teach young pharmacists, and fortunately for me, he invested a lot of time in teaching me. I gladly received all his instruction, and as an impressionable young man, interpreted the investment of his time to mean he thought I had potential.

During our training sessions, I mentioned to him on several occasions that I really wanted to go to medical school after I completed the pharmacy curriculum. He was very supportive and encouraged me to apply. As is still true today, the first step then in applying to medical school was to take a standardized test called the Medical College Admission Test (MCAT). I told Mr. Beeber I was going to take the MCAT, and he was very enthused about the possibility of one of his students eventually becoming a physician. He went so far as to purchase an MCAT study guide to assist me in preparing for the test. I took the test in Cincinnati and did very well, such that my scores on the MCAT put me in an excellent position to gain acceptance to medical school.

Because I was only in the first year of a three-year pharmacy program, taking the test with two years left gave me plenty of time to apply to medical school. Having this luxury of time, I decided to apply to the University of Cincinnati College of Medicine's early decision program. The benefit of applying early decision was that I would know very early if I was accepted and could make plans accordingly. The negative, however, was that I could apply to only one school, since a favorable admission decision would be binding. My logic was that if I did not get accepted on my first try, I would still have a year to apply to other medical schools while completing my final year of pharmacy school.

When a letter arrived from UC, I was thrilled to open it and find that I had been accepted into the 1983 entering class. After telling my parents the good news, my next call was to Mr. Beeber. He was very excited for me, and it was clear he felt a sense of pride in this accomplishment as well. After all, he had helped me work toward my lifelong goal.

Since it had always been my intention to complete my pharmacy degree before going to medical school, I deferred my admission for one year, as was permitted by the University of Cincinnati College of Medicine. During my third and final year in the pharmacy program, I spent more time working at Beeber Pharmacy and learned much more about the business side of pharmacy, all the while growing in my respect for Mr. Beeber.

In the summer of 1984, after graduating and while waiting on the results of the State Pharmacy Board Examination (required to practice pharmacy) I began to doubt whether going to medical school was the right decision for me. I talked with my parents and friends, but probably most importantly to Mr. Beeber. We spent a great deal of time discussing the pros and cons of a career in medicine versus a career in pharmacy. He made it very clear that he was proud of what I had accomplished, and no matter what I decided to do, he would support me. Many times during that summer, Mr. Beeber would say things like, "No matter what you decide, you will be successful," and "Both medicine and pharmacy are honorable professions. You can be proud of either one."

Like many others faced with a life-changing decision, I delayed the decision as long as I could, and it wasn't until the Friday before medical school was to start that I decided not to enroll. I called UC's College of Medicine to let them know I would not be attending. While they were very surprised at my decision, they replied that I had made some student on the waiting list a very happy person! Although it was a great relief to have made my decision, my next thought was, "Now what?" Having worked at Beeber for the past two-plus years while I was a student, I knew there were no pharmacist positions available there, so I would have to find a job. I spent Friday evening mulling over how I would tell Mr. Beeber I wasn't going to be a doctor after all. Despite his encouragement to take either path, I expected him to be disappointed that I wouldn't be going to medical school.

I went in to work the next day (I was a licensed pharmacist at this point), and told Mr. Beeber with some trepidation that I had decided not to attend medical school. Much to my surprise, he offered me a position on the spot to work as a staff pharmacist. Moreover, he was visibly enthused that I would be staying on! To Mr. Beeber's credit, once I informed him of my decision, he never mentioned medical school the rest of that day, or at any time after that day. He would later tell me that he wanted me to do what I felt was best for me, but if I didn't pursue medicine, he had plans for me at Beeber Pharmacy. In the ensuing years, we talked several times about his support of my decision. He spoke about the importance of encouraging others to seek their own way, even if it differs from what you want, so long as they are working toward something positive.

Throughout my career, many people have entered my organization and then moved on. Some of those people have gone on to do great things, whether in long-term care pharmacy or other fields. It is always sad to see good performers move on—after all, they make a manager's life easier and add to the company's success. There is something very satisfying, however, when there is that right "fit" between and an employer and an employee, resulting in a win for both sides. On that Saturday while standing in the pharmacy dispensing area, I can still remember Mr. Beeber saying, "Jeff, you will not regret this decision." He was right. I never have.

CHAPTER 3

"You dress like crap!"

I was a newly minted pharmacist, now with a full-time position at Beeber Pharmacy. As a fairly introverted person, I was aware that being a pharmacist would require me to interact with other health care professionals, and in most settings, the general public. In landing my position at Beeber Pharmacy, which focused on serving long-term care facilities, I managed to find a job that would limit my interaction with the public—something I considered a win for me! At the same time, I knew there would be significant interactions with the nurses and physicians providing health care in our clients' nursing facilities. Since I believed I had a very solid understanding of clinical pharmacy, I was confident I would be able to interact effectively with these professionals on a technical level.

In looking back at this time in my life, I have come to understand that I managed my discomfort with certain social situations by dressing in a manner that many would call flamboyant. At this time, proper attire for a male pharmacist was a shirt and tie along with a short white coat. Women wore the same kind of coat with their business attire. At the time I was hired, we had four male pharmacists and one female pharmacist.

Mr. Beeber was a fairly understated dresser and didn't pay a lot of attention to his appearance; while always professionally dressed, he did not have an extensive wardrobe, to say the least. At the time, leisure suits were popular, and he wore them often. One sign of his indifference to fashion was that he never spent much time coordinating his belt and shoe color, and it was not uncommon for him to have on a brown belt while wearing black shoes. I always coordinated my belt with my shoes, but I didn't stop there, as I would come into the pharmacy with some very interesting clothing ensembles. I had purple shirts, pink shirts, bright yellow shirts, and multicolor striped shirts, as well as what could only be described as an "interesting" array of pants. My pants colors included white, pastel blue, yellow, green, and some other colors that I now find difficult to describe. Suffice it to say that both then and now, they were "way outside the box." I remember thoroughly enjoying mixing and matching these colors and throwing in an unconventional tie to come up with what seemed like an attractive, colorful outfit to wear in the pharmacy.

In the LTC pharmacy business, there are two phases of work: the work done within the pharmacy to coordinate and fill prescriptions, and the clinical work performed at the nursing facilities being serviced by the LTC pharmacy. At this time, I was only working inside the pharmacy and had not yet begun to provide clinical consultant services at our clients' nursing facilities. Mr. Beeber and another staff pharmacist did all of the consulting, as the business was modest in size and was not growing very rapidly. I did, however, want to be a clinical consultant pharmacist and work in our facilities, as this is where I felt my clinical skills could best be utilized. As an introverted newcomer, however, I was not ready to move into this role, and I believe Mr. Beeber knew it. Although he had confidence in my clinical acumen, many times coming to me on the more complex pharmaceutical issues he encountered, he was very hesitant to put me in the field as consultant pharmacist. I was soon to find out why.

One day when Mr. Beeber returned to the pharmacy after working at a nursing home, I asked him, "Mr. Beeber, I have been here for three months. When are you going to let me consult?" At the time, I think I was wearing white pants, a pink shirt with a bright-colored tie, and of course my white lab coat. He quickly answered, "How about we discuss that tomorrow when I haven't been out consulting all day?" I agreed and was eager to talk the next day about getting involved in our clinical business. True to form, I arrived the next day in an outfit just as outrageous as the one I had been wearing the day before. I was the "opening pharmacist" that day, which meant I came in at 7:00 a.m. to get the day moving operationally. I was especially motivated to make sure the pharmacy was ahead of schedule when Mr. Beeber was due to arrive at 9:00 a.m. I remember being eager for him to arrive and wanting to have everything running smoothly. When he walked in, I immediately asked him when we could talk about clinical consulting. Much to my surprise he said, "Jeff, I think we should talk now." Mr. Beeber asked another staff pharmacist to watch the pharmacy operations for a few minutes while he and I spoke.

We went into a small office in the back where Mr. Beeber occasionally went to work on business matters. I sat across from him, noticing his signature leisure suit and brown belt with black shoes. He then proceeded with this very important lesson: "Jeff, you are a talented young man. You have all the tools to succeed in this business. You are smart, articulate, and have an honest way about you, but I have to tell you . . . YOU DRESS LIKE CRAP!!" He continued, "I can't let

19

you go into our customers' facilities looking like that. It's just not the professional image we want to portray."

'What?' I thought. 'My outfits are cool!' He then proceeded to tell me the importance of professional dress and how it makes an impression on people. He said I should not be using my work attire as a means of self-expression. "Let your talent and personality be what people notice," he said, "not the extravagance of your dress."

Mr. Beeber also said he understood I wanted to be involved clinically and affirmed he understood it was an important goal of mine. He said if I modified my attire, he would consider allowing me to go out into the field. All in all, he could not have been more supportive about helping me get better. "Please don't take this the wrong way," he said. "I only say these things because I want you to succeed."

As I left the pharmacy that day, I thought about how Mr. Beeber was always trying to help me and that I should not take offense. With only one more day before the weekend, I managed to choose some of my tamer pieces of clothing for work the next day. After thinking more about our talk, I knew I had some shopping to do over the weekend.

Sure enough, that weekend I went out and bought several conservative shirts, though still avoiding white ones! (To this day, I have never gotten comfortable in white shirts, and have found that most "white shirt" professionals I have worked with are less approachable.) I also purchased several pairs of pants in traditional colors, as well as some conservative ties. When I went in to work on Monday, decked out in my new wardrobe, the smile on Mr. Beeber's face was priceless. For weeks after our talk, when I would come in with my new conservative attire, he would give me a thumbs-up with that big, Beeber smile and say, "Now *that's* what I'm talking about!"

Shortly after this incident, Mr. Beeber put me right out in the field as a clinical consultant pharmacist. I practiced in this area for years, learning a great deal about the business and meeting people who would become professional contacts throughout my career. The fact that Mr. Beeber took the time to talk about something that was uncomfortable for him but made me a better employee made a lasting impression on me.

CHAPTER 4

"The Marketing Call"

Once my wardrobe had shaped up, I regularly spent a good portion of my days working as a clinical consultant pharmacist. This experience helped me overcome my introverted tendencies and become more comfortable working around a variety of people. I had already gained a strong foundation as an operations pharmacist, since by this time I had worked at Beeber Pharmacy for several years going back to my days as a student. I felt I had a thorough understanding of how our pharmacy worked and what was necessary to create a positive experience for our customers, and I had become quite familiar with the clinical aspects of our LTC pharmacy operation. It seemed like consulting and pharmacy operations were easier to get a handle on than the business development end of pharmacy services. I had yet to be involved in financial management, customer meetings (outside of clinical conferences), recruiting new customers, or any aspect of marketing.

After I had been a staff pharmacist for about a year, Mr. Beeber began taking me to customer meetings more and more. Usually I went as an observer, but occasionally he would call on me to discuss areas of operations I knew the most about within the pharmacy, or that he was less interested in. One meeting in particular was with our largest customer to discuss some issues they were having with their medical records. Mr. Beeber was truly a pioneer in medical record production for skilled nursing facilities, co-developing both the software and the medical record forms. Working with the medical records programs became a special interest of mine, and Mr. Beeber relied on me to manage this critical area for our customers.

At this particular meeting, we met with the CEO of the company and the VP of Professional Services, a nurse with significant experience in LTC and a true expert in medical care documentation in nursing homes. I was a little intimidated, to say the least, but the meeting went very well, and Mr. Beeber was pleased with the results. On the way back to the pharmacy, he was very complimentary of how I had handled myself, as he knew how nervous I had been leading up to the meeting. This experience boosted my confidence, as well as Mr. Beeber's faith in me to handle customer issues effectively. Although I didn't know it then, this nurse and I would go on to work together for almost twenty-five years. She is now a seasoned LTC executive in a senior leadership role in the LTC pharmacy industry.

Later that year, we received an RFP (Request for Proposal) from one of the largest nursing homes in Ohio. It was a huge opportunity, and I knew this could be a great customer for us if we were able to prevail in securing the business. I had never even seen an RFP before and was shocked by the amount of work it would take to complete it. Nonetheless, I immediately went to Mr. Beeber and presented it to him so I could get his ideas about how to proceed. When I showed him the RFP, much to my disappointment, he stated, "Jeff, they have been with the same pharmacy for 20 years, and we have no chance of getting that business." I wondered how this could be, so I inquired further. He explained the intricate working relationships within the facility and with the owner of the pharmacy that had the account, as well as some political issues in the county in which the facility was located. Given all these factors, he felt there was virtually no chance we would be successful.

So as to not totally dampen my spirits about the possibility of picking up this sizable account, he suggested I put together our response, allow him to review it, and then forward it to the customer and see what response we would receive. I had 60 days from the date we received the packet to gather the necessary materials and complete the customer's questionnaire. Knowing it was going to be a great deal of work, and having already been informed by Mr. Beeber that this was not to be done during my regular work day, I set aside time in the evenings to complete the response. Within about 30 days, I had completed the work, so I scheduled an appointment with Mr. Beeber to go over the proposal that I had prepared. He reviewed the proposal and complimented me on the thoroughness of the response. While being pleased with my work, he again cautioned me, "Jeff, in my opinion, we have no chance to get this business, so don't be disappointed if you don't even hear from them after we send in the response to the RFP." He knew how much time I had put in, so he added, "No matter what the result, this was a good experience for you and I'm proud of what you have put together." The response was sent to the customer the next day and then the waiting game began.

A few weeks later, I was working in the pharmacy and was paged to take a call. I was very surprised to hear the voice of the executive director and primary decision maker for the potential account thanking me for putting together such a thorough response to the RFP. We had a nice conversation about his facility and what they were looking for, and we discussed how Beeber Pharmacy might offer a solution for certain areas of concern. Most importantly, he informed me that we were one of three finalists (including the incumbent pharmacy, which Mr. Beeber thought could not be supplanted), and he asked if we could schedule a three-hour presentation at their facility later that month to present our proposal and answer questions. I responded we would be honored to do so and wrote down the date and time we were scheduled to meet with their board of directors, administrator, director of nursing, and executive director. I was elated at the prospect of telling Mr. Beeber we had made it to the final three and were scheduled to make a full-blown presentation. As I saw it, my work was over, and now it was up to Mr. Beeber to "make the sale." To my dismay, he was less than impressed and reiterated, "We aren't going to get the business, Jeff. They are just doing this because they want to put pressure on the current pharmacy."

Despite his reservations, Mr. Beeber agreed he would meet me at the facility on the appointed day to make the presentation. He was clear that it would be up to me to create the ancillary materials we would need, allow him to preview them before production, make the required number of copies, and have them at the facility on the date of the presentation. Since this was long before PowerPoint presentations, all of the visual aids had to be made manually. I photocopied many documents because I felt it was important that this potential new customer see details and real documents rather than descriptive summaries, especially in the areas of pricing, medical records, and clinical services. Following Mr. Beeber's careful review of everything we prepared to take to our presentation, we were ready to go.

For days leading up to the presentation, I teased Mr. Beeber about how it was "on him now" and that he better not blow this deal. This was going to be the first time I got to see Mr. Beeber in action trying to get new business, and I knew it was going to be a great learning experience. While I was still hoping I could drum up a little more enthusiasm in him, I was confident he would do well, given I had seen him in front of our current customers by now on several occasions, and his demeanor was always one of a confident expert. As we approached the presentation date, my anticipation was building.

On the day of the presentation, I left the pharmacy at 9:00 a.m. sharp for a 1:00 p.m. meeting an hour away. I was taking no chances on anything going wrong! Mr. Beeber had told me the day before, "Jeff, I am going to be up that way doing some consulting, so I will meet you at the facility rather than come back here." I arrived in town at 10:30 a.m. and went to a local restaurant to review the materials yet again and to relax prior to the presentation. About noon I left the restaurant and drove to the parking lot of the facility, just in time to see staff of the "other" pharmacy leaving after making their presentation. I knew it would be to our advantage to follow at least one other pharmacy, so seeing them leave ahead of our presentation was a confidence builder. At 12:30 p.m., I grabbed my box of materials and went inside to set up. The customer had told me I would have from 12:30 until 1:00 to set up, and I wanted to take advantage of every minute allotted. I dutifully placed packets around the table for all who would attend, plus extra copies for Mr. Beeber and me. It was now about 12:45 and Mr. Beeber was nowhere to be found. By this time, I was very nervous about his late arrival, and since this was before the advent of cell phones, I had no way to contact him. I could only wait and hope.

The executive director came over to greet me, and I assured him we were prepared to make our presentation and that Mr. Beeber would be joining me but hadn't arrived yet. The director made it clear that they expected to start at 1:00 sharp, which I acknowledged would not be a problem. When it was 12:55 and Mr. Beeber still was not there, the reality hit that I might have to do this presentation by myself. Surely something must be wrong, I thought. I could not imagine Mr. Beeber missing this meeting. It came time for our presentation, and Beeber or no Beeber, the show had to go on. I am sure there have been times in my career when I was more nervous, but I can't recall any even to this day. I stumbled through the presentation doing the best I could—no doubt amateurish at best—but I knew the material well and by this time understood how things worked in the pharmacy enough to answer all the questions asked of me.

After the presentation finished and we said our goodbyes, I felt dejected, thinking that not having Mr. Beeber there had really hurt our chances. Also, by now I was really worried that something bad had happened to him. Dispirited, I drove back to the pharmacy and was dumbfounded to see Mr. Beeber's yellow Volvo station wagon in the parking lot of the pharmacy. 'What was he thinking?' I asked myself. I walked into the pharmacy, and there he was, working away, filling prescriptions behind the counter. "Mr. Beeber, we had the big presentation today and you didn't show up! What happened?" He looked at me with that smile I had grown to appreciate for its genuineness and said, "Jeff, we have no chance to get that business, but

I thought it would be a good experience for you to handle the process from start to finish so you will appreciate how hard growing this business can be." 'Really,' I thought to myself. He went on to explain that since I had done so much work in responding to the RFP and compiling the supplemental materials, he knew I would do fine in the presentation. At the time, I was more than a little offended he had stood me up, but now, looking back, I think he saw this as an opportunity to force me out of my comfort zone. What better chance would there be for me to practice making a presentation when he felt we had no chance of winning the business?

Within a few weeks, I got the surprise of my early professional life when we learned that we were the successful respondent and were going to get the business! I will never forget the day we received that letter and the look on Mr. Beeber's face when he read it. He was truly shocked and thrilled at the same time.

Securing this business was a real boost in confidence for me, especially because it helped me feel comfortable in settings that, to this point in my career, had been difficult for me. Mr. Beeber knew I needed experience in this area of the business, and while my performance was a bit awkward, forcing me to sink or swim actually minimized my anxiety since I had no chance to fret in advance. If I had known ahead of time that I was going to give that presentation singlehandedly, I doubt I would have slept for weeks leading up to it. Mr. Beeber knew that being able to make this kind of presentation was going to be an absolute prerequisite for success in the business as I moved through my career.

Sure enough, as time went on, there were few things I felt more comfortable doing than presenting our services to potential customers. Mr. Beeber played a significant role in developing this confidence during my early years by allowing me to attend meetings with him and then allowing me to work through what we affectionately called for years thereafter "the marketing call." The mere recollection of it always made him smile.

CHAPTER 5

Sharing the Credit; Shouldering the Blame

Mr. Beeber taught many of us about leadership, but only rarely by talking about it. To learn about leadership from Mr. Beeber, you only had to watch him. I could tell early on that he could teach me a lot about the characteristics of an effective leader.

Although my career would eventually take me to a much larger corporate setting than the one in which Mr. Beeber operated, the leadership qualities he embodied were pertinent and effective no matter where they were employed. Mr. Beeber was not in any way a dictatorial leader; in fact, he led in a collaborative and, for the most part, calm way. Many days, when the pharmacy would be "on fire" busy, it never ceased to amaze me how calm he remained as we filled the days' orders in a timely manner and prepared for delivery to our client nursing facilities. When the work was the most intense, he was the most calm.

One evening, after a very busy Tuesday in the pharmacy (back in the late 1980s this was the busiest day of the week due to the procedures in place at that time), I remember asking him how he could stay calm when we were busiest, and when anxiety had a tendency to run at its highest. He said very succinctly, "Jeff, when things get the most hectic, when there is the most pressure or stress, <u>that</u> is the time when the leader needs to be most calm. If he or she is not, the entire team loses confidence in its leader." Occasionally Mr. Beeber would get upset when dealing with a problem, or with pharmacy employees, but NEVER during a hectic time. In the few instances when he had these minor outbursts, I figured he, too, needed a way to relieve his stress, but he only did so when appropriate to the situation and during a down time for the pharmacy.

Another way Mr. Beeber practiced leadership was by modeling a prodigious work ethic that his employees then tried to live up to. He was simply an incredibly hard worker, instilling a sense of urgency and a commitment to delivering services on time and exceeding customer expectations. He reminded all of us how important it was to understand and execute the "grunt" aspects of the LTC pharmacy business, and he did that by taking on a lot of the "grunt" work himself.

Beeber Pharmacy was always a team company. I cannot recall Mr. Beeber ever telling me what *he* did; it was always about what the team or *we* did. The more time I spent in business, the rarer I understood this quality to be. There is no shortage of leaders who talk about giving their team credit for success, but when most of them are in a situation where they can choose to give credit where credit is due or take credit for themselves, they choose the latter. During one of my rare conversations with Mr. Beeber on this topic, he told me, "When there is a failure, a leader should be the first in line to take the blame for it, but last in line when there is a success." The following example shows exactly what I mean.

Mr. Beeber and I were the only two pharmacists on duty one day and we were pretty busy. Since I was still fairly new, I'm sure I wasn't pulling my weight as we moved through the day. I ended up on a phone call with a nurse who was particularly argumentative about how a situation should be handled, and I was absolutely sure she was not correct in her assessment of the situation. As the conversation progressed, Mr. Beeber could tell that my tone did not match his expectations for customer service. At about this same time, the nurse asked me to "spell your first and last name for me because I want to report this situation to Mr. Beeber." I proceeded to begin spelling my name and Mr. Beeber motioned for me to let him speak with the nurse. I told the nurse that Mr. Beeber was in the pharmacy and asked if she would like to speak with him. She answered affirmatively, so I passed the phone over to him.

I was interested to see how he was going to handle the situation, so I stayed close enough to hear his side of the conversation. At first he listened intently, taking some notes and then responding in a way that resolved the issue to her satisfaction. I will never forget what happened next. While still on the phone, he looked directly at me and said, "Nurse, I apologize for you feeling that Jeff was disrespectful to you on the phone. You know that is not acceptable here at my pharmacy. Jeff is a new pharmacist and has not spent as much time on the phone with our nurses as the rest of us, and I have not given him sufficient training on how to handle calls with all of our customers. You can be sure I will give him the extra training he needs so this does not happen in the future." I remember thinking, 'He is totally taking the hit for me like it is his fault. Why would he do that?'

As soon as Mr. Beeber hung up the phone, he proceeded to let me know, in no uncertain terms, that what he had just done would not happen again. "Jeff, you made that mistake for the first time and I took the blame for it. If you do it again, you won't be working for Beeber Pharmacy any longer. Am I clear on this?" I told him I understood, apologized for putting him in that situation, and made a mental note that losing my cool with a customer would never happen again. I remember feeling bad about this situation, but I felt empowered because he stood up for me when he could have focused on my error and not about his commitment to leadership and customer service. I never put him in that situation again, but I also knew if I made a mistake of a different type because of my inexperience or knowledge deficiency, he would be there to support me.

Throughout my career, and especially in the later years of my career in LTC pharmacy, I heard many people talk about being leaders, but few of them ever backed up their words. It was trendy to talk about, and I am sure they fancied themselves as powerful leaders, but the reality was they were usually out for themselves and would rarely hesitate to "throw others under the bus" if it would make them look better. Some of these were my supervisors, and I knew they did not support me when I wasn't in the room. How did I know this? All too often, I saw them disparage or blame others for situations that were their own fault because they could do so without any retribution. If they were willing to do this to other loyal employees, then surely they were doing it to me as well.

Real leaders are supportive in your presence and most importantly, behind your back, and they never let you take the blame alone (except in rare cases of malfeasance). Also, real leaders recognize that making mistakes and learning from them is how employees get better. If you find yourself working for this kind of leader, consider yourself lucky, because such a person is rare indeed.

CHAPTER 6

The Joy of Giving

After I graduated from pharmacy school, like most students, I had college debt. Mr. Beeber spoke to me early on about the importance of paying off this debt before I made any significant purchases. Additionally, my father reviewed my first paycheck as a pharmacist and gave me similar advice. My father also counseled me to begin saving money right away since I didn't need my whole paycheck to cover living expenses. I knew both men had given me sound advice, so my first order of business was to pay off my student loan in about eight months. (As I recall, it was about $4,000.) I was able to save a small amount of money in addition to making the loan repayment, so I felt pretty good about finally being able to buy a brand new car.

I suppose every young person dreams of his or her first "new car," and I was no different. I spent weeks researching which car I was most interested in, and as one might expect, I did what any recent college graduate with a little bit of money saved up would do: I bought a shiny, red, 1985 Pontiac Trans Am. Although it was a trendy car at the time, it was also about the most impractical car one could ever think about purchasing. The back seats were cramped, and it had terrible gas mileage—but it was cool!

I vividly remember driving up to the pharmacy on a Monday after having picked up the car on Saturday, feeling very proud of my new vehicle. Life was good! Mr. Beeber, in his trusty Volvo station wagon, happened to follow me into the parking lot. He saw me emerge from the car and came by to look it over. He walked all around the car, noting its various features, and then glanced around the interior. After his inspection, he looked at me and said, "Jeff, that is a really nice car. I bet it is exciting to drive, isn't it?" 'He likes it,' I thought to myself. I agreed with him that it was very exciting to drive, and said getting a new car was something I had really been looking forward to. I had told him a few weeks earlier about my student loan being paid off, so he knew I had taken his advice before making this large purchase. He looked around a little more, and then we both went into the pharmacy to begin the workday.

As the days went by, I was enjoying owning the new vehicle, but not enjoying the amount of money I was spending on gas. Also, I was not too thrilled about the cost of something I had not checked into very closely: insurance. Nonetheless, I was having fun with something I had always wanted and felt I had been responsible in waiting until I had paid off my student loan and saved a bit of money before buying the new car.

About four weeks after I purchased my new car, Mr. Beeber, once again, followed me into the parking lot, came over to the car and asked, "How are things with the car?" I told him things were good, and that I was pleased with my new vehicle. He looked at me and said, "Not quite the same as it was when you first got it, now is it?" Not giving me time to answer, he proceeded into the pharmacy to begin the day, with me following behind, pondering what he had said. As lunch time approached, Mr. Beeber invited me to join him for lunch, stating, "I have something important to discuss with you." Not thinking too much about it, I accepted his invitation, and we agreed to meet in the fast-food restaurant next door.

Lunchtime came and we sat down in the restaurant after ordering our food. Initially, we talked about the day's events and how busy we were at the pharmacy—nothing close to the "something important to discuss with you" I had been expecting. We were approaching the end of our meal when Mr. Beeber suddenly stopped, put down his sandwich, and began to discuss what he had clearly come to talk about. "Jeff, how is the new car doing? Seriously, is it not just a vehicle to get you from point A to point B now that the newness has worn off?" I thought about his question for a minute and then responded how I understood what he meant and yes, the newness had worn off to a degree and therefore it was not as exciting as when I first got the car. I asked whether this wasn't a normal feeling with any new purchase after some time had passed. His expression got very serious, and he looked me in the eye and said, "Jeff, I want you to listen to me very carefully. You will never buy anything for yourself that brings you happiness. You will however, buy things for others that will bring you lifelong joy. Please don't forget this." With that, he put down the rest of his sandwich, rolled it up in its wrapper so he could throw it away, and left without saying another word. I remember thinking, 'That's crazy! Of course I will buy things that will make me happy.' Now that some years have passed, it turns out Mr. Beeber was right.

Mr. Beeber was telling me never to allow myself to become materialistic or to put my personal desires above those of others who are important to me. He knew that true satisfaction from material success comes only when we use our resources to contribute to the happiness and well-being of others. Whether we buy things for those close to us or support philanthropic causes benefiting people we don't know, we experience the greatest satisfaction with money when we don't spend it on ourselves.

To this day, I still enjoy buying a new vehicle every few years, but each time I drive out of the dealership, I smile as I think about what Mr. Beeber told me at lunch that day. Invariably I arrive home and have the same thought: I wonder why I just traded in a vehicle that I liked and was almost identical to this one?

I have been fortunate to be able to travel with family and friends to some really great places. I have also been able to provide things for my family and friends because of opportunities that have come my way and have brought me a level of financial success. Each time I see others enjoying what I have been fortunate enough to be able to give, I feel a much greater sense of joy than with anything I have ever done for myself or bought for myself.

Of all the lessons Mr. Beeber taught me, this is the one I cherish the most. It has proven to be true time and time again without fail. Buy something for someone else and see how much joy it brings you. For this lesson I will be eternally grateful.

CHAPTER 7

Home Care Pharmacy of Florida

As the summer of 1985 approached, I had been with Mr. Beeber for three years, with the last one of those as a licensed pharmacist. I was enjoying getting to know the business more in depth, and Mr. Beeber's confidence in my abilities continued to rise. Our working relationship could not have been better.

One evening after the pharmacy closed, our conversation drifted to my career goals now that I had decided to stay in pharmacy as my profession. Mr. Beeber and I discussed my current objectives, which were to hone my skills in operations, obtain more clinical experience, and ultimately get more involved in the pharmacy's management. He supported all these aspirations, but was eager to offer another suggestion. Mr. Beeber and three of his business associates were thinking about starting an LTC pharmacy in Orlando, Florida, and they wanted to know if I would be interested in being a partner and managing this start-up business. I was flattered to be considered for this opportunity, but apprehensive at the same time. Mr. Beeber and his partners were accomplished, successful businessmen with significant experience. I had been out of pharmacy school for just a year and had relatively little business development or management experience. Mr. Beeber and I agreed I would give it some thought and we would talk later.

After thinking about it for only a few days, I decided this would be a great opportunity and told Mr. Beeber as much. I would own a small part of the pharmacy (sweat equity), and would have solid partners with great LTC pharmacy acumen who could "rescue" me if something unexpected arose. I was still very clinical at this point in my career, so I anticipated that it would not be difficult for me to pass the Florida State Board of Pharmacy Exam. With this certification, I could be the pharmacist in charge (a requirement for all licensed pharmacies) of the new pharmacy we were going to create. The name of the pharmacy would be Home Care Pharmacy of Florida, which coincided with a pharmacy in Ohio in which Mr. Beeber was also involved. The partners and I agreed the Florida entity would benefit from the excellent reputation of Home Care Pharmacy in Ohio.

After several months of planning and hard work, the pharmacy opened in December 1985. Thanks to Mr. Beeber's training, I was familiar with doing "grunt" work, all of which fell to me as the only pharmacist on duty. It proved to be a great deal of work to get this venture off the ground, but starting from scratch was an invaluable experience and taught me many things about the pharmacy business that would be extremely useful later in my career.

To help our pharmacy grow, we engaged another partner whose experience was in nursing and who had a great deal of expertise in the sales and marketing area. Our general plan was that I would concentrate on operations and she would handle business development, nursing issues, and client/customer relations. This fit well with my personality, as I knew I could take care of the business if she was able to generate it. It turned out she was very good at speaking with people, but getting them to commit to the new business was not her strong suit. It became clear to me that if we were going to grow the business, I would have to find a way to contribute in this area as well.

After several months of less than satisfactory results on the sales front, I asked for and received some assistance from my accomplished business associates back in Ohio. They provided voluminous amounts of marketing materials for me to "modify" to fit the Florida market, gave me copies of their presentation packets, and were more than generous with advice about various ways to convince customers to do business with Home Care Pharmacy of Florida instead of with our more seasoned competitors.

I took the materials provided by the group and developed a marketing packet that could be customized based upon the needs of a particular customer (skilled nursing facility, assisted living residence, group home, etc.). I felt the packet would generate some interest if I could get it into the right hands. Since I had to be in the pharmacy every day to take care of the one customer we had, I knew I would be limited in the number of sales calls I could make and therefore had to make each of them as fruitful as possible. Additionally, I needed to qualify the customers before reaching out because any call to an account we had no chance of getting was simply a waste of time. In light of this immense time crunch, I put together a very concise sales plan for the targeted few. This exercise was not easy given my lack of experience, but building a sales plan gave me perspective on qualifying customers, which taught me a great deal about business development in the LTC pharmacy business and served me well later in my career.

The sales plan was executed over several months, and while we had some success in attracting new clients, there was not enough business for me to be relieved of the daily dispensing functions, or to share on-call duties. As the only pharmacist, I was on call 24/7 for many months since we simply could not afford additional coverage. Although the on-call volume was fairly low, it was nonetheless exhausting to never get a true break from the business.

At the same time we were launching this pharmacy, I was starting my married life, having been married in December 1985. Starting both a new business and a new marriage proved much more challenging than I had anticipated. I was working an inordinate number of hours running the pharmacy, and was trying to grow the business in my off hours. It was not long before things became difficult for my wife. Finally, one evening it came out that she wanted to go back to Ohio. It simply was not working out for her in Florida. Whether her feelings were due to the number of hours I was putting in or the natural loneliness one feels when getting established in a new city, either way I knew something had to change.

I also knew my business partners, most especially Mr. Beeber, were going to be bitterly disappointed if and when I approached them about moving back to Ohio and no longer managing the pharmacy in Florida. I worried for weeks about how to discuss this with them; finally, I decided to approach just Mr. Beeber instead of the entire group. I was concerned my career with Mr. Beeber might come to an end, and I would need to look for another job in Ohio. Nonetheless, I felt it was the right thing to do for my family, which was more important to me than my job. I remember thinking, 'How can he not just get rid of me? He is going to be so disappointed in me.' The time for the discussion was drawing near and I was dreading it more than words can describe.

Finally, having committed to my wife to call prior to a certain date and when I could delay no longer, I nervously placed the call to Mr. Beeber. "Mr. Beeber, I have something I need to discuss with you," I said. He listened, and I know he could tell something was wrong. "This is not working out for my family and I am going to have to come back to Ohio. I can't stay here in Florida. I'm sorry." There was silence on the phone for several seconds and then Mr. Beeber said the following: "Jeff, you have to do what is right for your family first. The pharmacy here has been going downhill since you left, so if you want to come back, I would love to have you back to manage the pharmacy on one condition." "Sure. What is that?" I said. "You must find your replacement before you come back to Ohio so the partners are not left in a bad position." I told him I understood and assured him I would find my replacement before I moved back to Ohio. I was stunned. Not only did he not seem disappointed, he actually seemed excited about having me come back to manage the pharmacy. This was too good to be true!

It was not difficult to find a replacement for my position since the pharmacy was beginning to grow. It was a great opportunity for an entrepreneurial pharmacist. I found a talented person to take over, and then spent about 30 days training him before moving back to Ohio. I was elated to take over as Beeber Pharmacy's director, particularly since I was concerned my career at Beeber would be over when I resigned my partnership in the Florida venture.

Mr. Beeber knew how hard I had been working, as he had observed it firsthand. It would have been easy for him to find someone else to run his pharmacy in Ohio and simply let me go. He later told me he respected how I had hung in there when I wasn't happy, and given the right situation, he knew I could help him get Beeber Pharmacy back on track.

While I had been away, the operations at Beeber had fallen into disrepair, with no one spending time on the basic parameters of the business. Pricing and billing irregularities were beginning to create issues with both customers and payers. Mr. Beeber knew I was adept at this kind of detailed work, and I could tell he was glad I was available to help him get the pharmacy operations back in order. This was my first experience in a pharmacy environment where the "grunt details"—as Mr. Beeber used to refer to them—had not been appropriately monitored. During this period, Mr. Beeber basically gave me free reign in designing and implementing the internal operational procedures. At 26 years of age, I was not a likely candidate to be in charge of pharmacy operations, but by this time Mr. Beeber trusted my instincts, admired my work ethic, and knew this was not what he wanted to be doing. He wanted to focus on growing the business, so he put me in charge of running the day-to-day pharmacy operations, and informed the customers that we had made changes that would impact their experience for the better. He also began to create name recognition for me with the customers, with more and more of them asking for me by name when they called to inquire about a particular issue in their nursing facility. It did not take long for operations to improve once we attended to some important details.

Later in 1986, a young pharmacy student from the University of Cincinnati came to our pharmacy for her four-week externship. Her name was Gina Pruitt (nka Gina Timmons). Mr. Beeber felt it would be a good experience for me to be her preceptor, and I was eager to train another pharmacy student since I was recently out of school myself and felt I could help her learn both the clinical and operational aspects of LTC pharmacy. Gina was a very intelligent and confident student, and it became clear to me she was the type of pharmacist we wanted at Beeber. I made sure she knew that upon her graduation, we wanted her to consider Beeber Pharmacy for her first position. Fortunately for us, Gina did come to work for Beeber Pharmacy after graduation, and she remains one of the premier experts in the LTC pharmacy specialty today. Gina is a recognized expert in LTC pharmacy information technology, both within her current company and with health professionals throughout the LTC industry. Few people know how many senior leaders in the LTC pharmacy industry have or had direct roots to Beeber Pharmacy in its humble strip mall in Trotwood, Ohio. There is likely no single pharmacy entity in the United States that has produced more leaders in the industry.

Mr. Beeber was committed to the education of young pharmacists and considered it an honor to participate in their development. He was a phenomenal teacher because he understood the importance of developing the next generation of leaders in his pharmacy specialty—a specialty he essentially created. He had a unique ability to identify talented people and train them in how to maintain the highest level of customer satisfaction.

CHAPTER 8

A Man of His Word

As previously mentioned, Beeber Pharmacy's profitability slipped during the time I was in Florida. Mr. Beeber had been focusing on his strongest areas, which were customer service and attracting new clients to the LTC business, and no one was left in charge of applying the necessary scrutiny to day-to-day operations. When we agreed that I would return to Ohio, Mr. Beeber made his expectations clear to me: fix the operational issues and get the pharmacy back on the right track financially. He also made it very clear that he trusted me and would support the changes necessary to accomplish our goals.

Back in 1986, margins in the LTC pharmacy business were quite robust; in fact, the earnings of Beeber Pharmacy the year I left for Florida were comparable to the gross margins in the business today. Despite those favorable market conditions, in a span of less than 18 months, Beeber went from being a significantly profitable business with excellent cash flow to one with marginal profitability and mediocre cash flow. As I began to examine invoices and financial statements, the reasons for this downturn became obvious to me. At the same time, I was surprised by others' lack of understanding as to why the pharmacy was not succeeding. My analysis of Beeber's predicament taught me two valuable lessons. First, you must always pay attention to even the smallest details of your business, and second, you must have managers who understand how each component of the business contributes to the success (or failure) of the whole. Although this sounds quite basic, I have watched expert manager after expert manager fail because they simply did not understand their own business or know how the various parts impacted the entire operation. Mr. Beeber was a stickler for having his pharmacists know the entire business. His demand that each of us in his employ understand all aspects of our responsibilities made us better executives as we moved through our careers.

One of my first tasks was to review Beeber's gross profit report. Stated simply, this report lists every item sold the previous month and presents the percentage and dollar margins for each item. Since Beeber sold thousands of different products, this was a voluminous report, and it was very tedious to study it. Nonetheless, it was essential to do so, since it allowed a manager to flag any items for which the pharmacy was not getting sufficient reimbursement. Prior to leaving for Florida, I had reviewed this report monthly and had often adjusted pricing as needed to keep the margins at the levels Mr. Beeber and I agreed were appropriate. As far as I could tell, not a single person had reviewed it the whole time I was away. Mr. Beeber's business partner felt he was quite adept at managing the price schedules of the pharmacy, however, he had taken several short cuts when determining the pricing. One of these was to fix the price of medication regardless of payer; another was to prevent any price updates from being done automatically, as was the practice at the time. As a result, some drugs provided in very high volumes were being sold below the pharmacy's actual acquisition cost! I recall sharing my findings with Mr. Beeber, and he said with exasperation, "Well, Jeff, if you are selling drugs below cost, you sure can't make it up on volume! I hope you will remember this." By this time, I was well past needing him to tell me this, but I did appreciate him saying, "Jeff, I'm glad you're back. You pay attention to the details more than anyone who has ever worked for me, and this is why I trust you to run my pharmacy!" There are few things I can recall Mr. Beeber saying that made me feel better than hearing that he trusted me. I remember feeling very proud when he made that statement to me.

When Mr. Beeber and I had first discussed my return as manager, I was unaware of the extent of the problems that had developed in my absence. Mr. Beeber had no obligation to tell me about them in any detail, and for whatever reason, he didn't do so. What Mr. Beeber did do was discuss how important this pharmacy was to him. He noted that putting me in charge of the pharmacy would be questioned by his partner and others, but if I was successful in turning things around, he would pay me a cash bonus in a specified amount. I had never had a cash bonus (or any other type of bonus) at this point in my career, so I had no concept of how it should be structured or what would be fair. I trusted Mr. Beeber to look out for my best interests and the business interests of Beeber Pharmacy.

For the rest of 1986, I worked very hard to get the pharmacy back to the level of profitability Mr. Beeber had previously enjoyed. In addition to adjusting price schedules, I had to address the various billing issues contributing to cash flow problems for the pharmacy. Due to billing errors, submission errors, and write-offs, the pharmacy was not getting paid as it should have, and cash flow suffered accordingly.

By the end of the year, the pharmacy was back to being profitable and was even adding new customers. All in all the year was a good one, but cash flow was still a problem. From my analysis and my monthly meetings with Mr. Beeber, I knew there was not sufficient cash to pay bonuses to the employees as Mr. Beeber had intended. For the first time, Mr. Beeber asked me to review the year-end bonuses with him. He walked into the meeting room, sat down, looked directly at me, and said, "Jeff, you know we don't have the money to pay the bonuses we had intended to pay, however, you've earned the bonus I committed to you when you agreed to come back and run the pharmacy. You have done a great job and I want you to have this." He then proceeded to slide an envelope across the table containing a check for the entire amount he had committed to me.

Since I was well aware the pharmacy could not afford this much, I knew he had used his own money to pay my bonus and the bonuses of the other employees. To my knowledge, Mr. Beeber took no bonus from the operation of the pharmacy that year. It was just like him to make a personal sacrifice so he could fulfill his commitments to others. I later asked him about this bonus and he told me he knew his small sacrifice would come back tenfold because it conveyed his appreciation for our collective efforts. Despite Mr. Beeber putting himself last in line to reap the rewards of his labors, I know he felt happy about giving the bonuses that year, because it was the perfect fulfillment of his philosophy of giving to others. He truly lived out his motto of gaining happiness by spending on others rather than himself.

Mr. Beeber was a practical, trustworthy man who understood how to motivate people appropriately. He was perhaps the most generous person with whom I ever worked. During my career, I witnessed astounding corporate greed—consumption without limits, with little to no recognition or compensation for those who contributed to senior executives' success. Each time I witnessed this kind of excess, I would think how unfortunate it was these executives had never been taught by Mr. Beeber that the true joy of success is when it is shared. Very late in my career, I had a brief opportunity to work with John Figueroa, CEO of Omnicare, Inc. John embodied many of the lessons Mr. Beeber espoused, and in his first year as CEO, John created an equitable bonus program for hundreds of employees. Watching the positive impact of this most basic and fair gesture on the morale of employees and the performance of the company reinforced what I had known for years: that sharing with others in a generous and equitable way works wonders in all companies regardless of their size.

CHAPTER 9

An Operator and a Clinician

Throughout the first few years of my employment, Mr. Beeber insisted that I become involved in both sides of the pharmacy business: clinical and operations. It was the norm within LTC pharmacy circles during this time for pharmacists to be involved in both aspects of the business, and for Mr. Beeber, they were inextricably connected. In his view, you could not be proficient at either one unless you understood both. On several occasions, he shared that he envisioned a day when consultant pharmacy (the clinical side) would become a subspecialty of the LTC pharmacy business. Should this happen, he said, it would become increasingly difficult for any one person to become an "expert" in the overall business. His vision eventually became a reality in the industry as many clinicians today are rarely, if ever, involved in the actual dispensing of prescriptions or the true operation of the pharmacy. Simply put, today's clinical pharmacists provide clinical evaluations in the LTC facilities; many rarely, if ever, work in their pharmacy in a dispensing role.

In the nursing home industry, each skilled nursing facility must have a licensed consultant pharmacist of record or an in-house pharmacy. In-house pharmacies are very rare because they are not cost justified. As a result, nearly all skilled nursing centers hire a consultant pharmacist to ensure compliance with clinical, administrative, and clerical regulations of their state health department.

Throughout the 1980s, Mr. Beeber made it a point to have each of his pharmacists work both outside the pharmacy as a consultant pharmacist and inside the pharmacy as an operations pharmacist. Because of this policy, each of us developed a keen understanding of the daily dispensing functions of the pharmacy, and more importantly, how any deficiency in operations negatively impacted our customers as they provided patient care at the skilled nursing facility. Additionally, by visiting our skilled nursing customers regularly, we developed the requisite relationships with customers at all levels. Mr. Beeber made it very clear that we were "responsible" to ensure the administrator, director of nursing, medical director, and staff nurses understood how we operated, and, more importantly, were happy with our services. If there was any inkling of dissatisfaction, it was our responsibility to get the issue resolved and to maintain a positive customer relationship. I believe Mr. Beeber's commitment to having his pharmacists be well rounded in all aspects of the business contributed significantly to his success. By including me in various meetings and other interactions, he intended to provide me with a holistic understanding of the entire business and not just one aspect.

In the LTC pharmacy industry, there is much discussion about "churn," meaning the "natural movement" of customers from one pharmacy provider to another. There was very little "churn" throughout my tenure with Mr. Beeber. His philosophy was that losing current customers was simply unacceptable, in large part because proper customer service made it preventable. He recognized that his business was, at its heart, relationship based, and by attending to the needs of his customers in a prompt, courteous fashion, those relationships could become long lasting.

Frankly, I was too young at the time I worked with Mr. Beeber to know whether he was right or wrong in insisting that pharmacists learn all sides of the business. As I later moved into executive positions, I spent a great deal of time with other executives who were "experts," many of whom took pride in negotiating contracts, developing plans of approach, implementing acquisition plans, or creating new policies and procedures. These "experts" routinely made mistakes that others who had a deeper understanding of the business had to correct. I will be forever grateful to Mr. Beeber for teaching me about the pharmacy business in a holistic manner. It was undoubtedly one of the most profound lessons he bestowed upon me.

CHAPTER 10

AccuCare Health Services Is Born

Before I knew it, I had been with Mr. Beeber for almost five years, and our professional relationship kept growing stronger. He continued to invest himself in my development, and I was more than eager to learn from him. The lesson that was about to unfold summed up, in many ways, the mutual respect and friendship we had built during our time together.

Part of my responsibilities in 1987 and 1988 included being the consultant pharmacist for a fairly large inner-city facility with a long history of caring for the indigent of Greater Dayton, Ohio. This consulting assignment would not have been considered a "top pick" among the staff pharmacists at Beeber. Since the facility was located in a high-crime area, Mr. Beeber insisted that one of the male pharmacists take on this duty, and as the male with lowest seniority, I drew the short straw. For many months after my assignment began, this facility struggled with retaining a director of nursing, even though it had a great staff of nurses who provided excellent care for the residents. After trying a couple of different nurses in this position, the administrator approached me with the news that he had hired a young, intelligent, and highly energetic director of nurses. Based on the description of the nurse soon to arrive, I felt she would be just what the facility, staff, and residents needed.

I remember meeting the new director, Cindy Heit (nka Cindy Heit-Welsh), for the first time and thinking, "Wow, she really is young and full of energy!" I came to find out that she had a very unusual skill set, in that she was empathetic with employees and patients, as well as uncommonly effective with the doctors, medical director, and staff nurses. Most uniquely, she possessed keen business acumen and was aware of how every person working in the facility (including me) impacted the quality of care and financial viability. The caregiving team Cindy led became one of the most effective I was ever involved in, and it became a model for how all the medical disciplines could come together to provide optimal care in a difficult environment.

I remember telling Mr. Beeber about Cindy, opining that she would not stay at this facility long because she was motivated to do bigger and better things. I knew of her aspirations from discussions we had while working together, as well as through a developing friendship my wife and I had with Cindy and her husband. During social visits we would discuss various business objectives, and I learned that she had goals well beyond what this facility could offer. It was during one of these social visits that she indicated she was going to be leaving the nursing facility to run a local nursing agency. While I was sad to hear she was leaving, I was glad to hear Cindy and her husband would be staying in Dayton and that she had a promising career opportunity.

Not long after Cindy took over at the nursing agency, she reached out to me and asked about my interest in being on her board of directors, as she needed a pharmacist on the board. I readily accepted, and the first couple of meetings I attended were uneventful. The third meeting was when we had the opportunity to review the budget. This was the first time I really had a chance to see the numbers of this business for myself. She had told me the business was very profitable, but I had no idea how profitable until we reviewed the budget. My experience working with Mr. Beeber enabled me to see that this business required little capital (unlike LTC pharmacy), and if you had the nurses, it was a pretty basic business model of supply and demand. It was all about getting nurses on board, and I had certainly seen Cindy's ability to do that even in the face of the nursing shortage of the late 1980s.

I approached Cindy after the meeting about potentially starting a business to do what her agency was doing. She indicated she had a fairly extensive non-compete agreement that would preclude her from participating in a similar business in Southwest Ohio. It was common, both then and now, for health care businesses that depended on professional relationship development and maintenance to have such agreements in place. I had one with Mr. Beeber, in fact, as it was standard practice. I was disappointed, yet not surprised, to hear about her non-compete agreement. We agreed we would continue to look for ways we could potentially get into this business.

I discussed the situation with Mr. Beeber and he offered an excellent idea. Mr. Beeber and I, along with his long-time business partner and several others, had invested to various degrees in a start-up LTC pharmacy in Dallas, Texas. Out of the blue, Mr. Beeber said, "Why not approach Cindy about starting a nursing agency in Dallas?" I remember thinking this was a great idea, but after thinking about my brief foray to Florida, I was not sure how she and her husband would feel about moving to a new state when all of their family lived in or around Dayton, Ohio. I called Cindy the next day to discuss the idea and she was sold on it, as was her husband! They loved the idea of a fresh new start in a new city, but mostly she was excited at the prospect of owning a significant part of a new company. I informed her that Mr. Beeber and his partner had already agreed to become our financial partners, and that I would call her in short order to go over a proposed structure for the venture and plan how we might proceed. I immediately called Mr. Beeber to tell him about Cindy's receptiveness to the idea of starting the business in Dallas.

Mr. Beeber, his partner, and I sat down and worked out the terms: Mr. Beeber and his partner would put up $50,000 each in equity, I would put up $30,000, and Cindy would put up no money since she represented the "sweat equity" partner. Because of Mr. Beeber's suggestion that I invest my own "sweat equity" by spending one week per month on the new venture, my financial contribution would be less than his. Mr. Beeber proposed that the two working partners (Cindy and I) would each own thirty percent, and Mr. Beeber and his partner would each own twenty percent. I presented this structure to Cindy, and she was ready to move forward with the deal. In so doing, AccuCare Health Services, Inc., was born.

We secured the necessary checks from the contributing partners, set up bank accounts, incorporated the business, and made plans to get the office set up. Cindy and I had a very positive working relationship throughout the beginning of this venture, with both of us very excited to be part of something new and potentially profitable. I knew her skill set well, and felt strongly she could not only attract the nurses to the business but could also negotiate with customers in a fair but firm way. The only area where Cindy really needed assistance was in business structure and accounting, so those were functions I took on. We found a great office site very close to the other business we had in Dallas and opened the doors in October 1989.

AccuCare Health Services was a temporary nursing agency, which in the late 1980s was a very viable business. Cindy recruited nurses, and those nurses were deployed as "temporary" nursing staff in the hospital, long-term care, and home health markets. During this period of time the United States had a significant nursing shortage, and businesses like AccuCare provided the nurses health care providers needed to provide the necessary continuum of care.

In our first month, we brought in less than $1,000 in sales, but it was evident Cindy had exceptional skill for attracting nurses (the driving force behind all sales) and new customers. Just as I had anticipated, she was a complete natural in developing the business, and while I was a novice at accounting, I knew enough to keep us appropriately directed financially. What no one had really expected, other than she and I, was the level of success we would have, and how quickly it would come. Cindy was bringing in nurses almost as fast as we could get them signed up, and the new customers (hospitals, long-term care facilities, and home health agencies) were literally lining up to consume the services we were offering. The more business Cindy attracted, the more confident she became, and by the spring of 1990, the business was really taking off.

Mr. Beeber watched the new business very closely, and we were in constant communication about it. He made it clear, however, that it was my responsibility to handle everything with Cindy. I could tell he was as pleased as I was with how well things had started. He cautioned me, though, by saying, "Jeff, this business looks like a fantastic business opportunity for all of us, but you must be careful." I inquired further about his concern, so he added, "We are growing very quickly, and you need to make sure the cash flow can keep up with our responsibilities to our employees. Too much success too fast can ruin the business, just as not enough business can." Cindy and I were about to learn this lesson firsthand, and at the same time gain a full appreciation of Mr. Beeber's trust in us.

By this time I was becoming more confident from a business perspective, not only in the LTC pharmacy business, but in ancillary businesses as well. Mr. Beeber had taught me the tenets of business, and by now I was stretching my legs a bit, infusing some of my own ideas with the backing of Mr. Beeber's full confidence. Still weighing carefully the comments he had made about cash flow and growth, I was being as cautious as I could be without dampening Cindy's spirits or hampering the growth of the new business.

The business continued to grow almost exponentially each month. By the beginning of summer, cash flow was barely covering the payroll from the previous week, and I desperately did not want to go back to Mr. Beeber to ask for money. Nonetheless, after a telephone discussion with Cindy, I found myself lying in bed on a Wednesday night, knowing we could not make payroll on Friday unless we received several large payments on Thursday from customers who had said they would pay. It was time for me to discuss the situation with Mr. Beeber and I knew it. I talked to Cindy in Texas, and she assured me that our accounts receivable were solid. If we needed to take out further loans, paying them back would not be an issue. Although I already knew this, it was still good to get a second opinion and gain some moral support before I talked to Mr. Beeber.

The next morning I went in to speak with Mr. Beeber, and almost before I opened my mouth he said, "We are out of money at AccuCare, aren't we, Jeff?" My response was a simple, "Yes, sir, we are." He asked me how much we needed to make payroll, and then inquired if the accounts receivable were good to cover it. I told him we needed $30,000, and that we had every reason to expect prompt payment by our customers.

I will never forget what happened next. He looked at me, put his hand on my shoulder and said, "Jeff, I trust Cindy and I trust you, and I can invest in you both with great confidence." I remember thinking about how gracious that statement was, particularly since I effectively had my hand out for a large sum of money. After years of reflection, I have come to believe that I have never felt better in my professional life than at that moment. Mr. Beeber had invested his time, money, and expertise in Cindy and me, and I believe it was during this time that he came to feel his investment was a wise one.

We discussed the situation more in depth, and Mr. Beeber decided to wire more than $30,000 so the business could be stabilized from a cash flow perspective. I am happy to say the business never had another cash call from that point forward.

What was also astounding to me is that Mr. Beeber wired the money without so much as a handwritten note that the business owed him the money. I don't recall a situation other than this one where Mr. Beeber did not clearly document his business activities. We eventually created a note to memorialize this "loan" to the company, but in the moment, Mr. Beeber showed me that a handshake from a trusted partner is reliable in and of itself.

CHAPTER 11

Omnicare Comes Calling

It was the winter of 1989, and business at Beeber Pharmacy was booming. Furthermore, our new business venture in Dallas, AccuCare Health Services, Inc., was growing monthly, with very high expectations for continued growth. Mr. Beeber was continuing to give me more and more responsibility with the business both internally and externally. I was having much more customer interaction than I had earlier in my career and was spending more and more time with Mr. Beeber in meetings with key customers. I always found these meetings to be informative from a business perspective, as well as valuable in developing the negotiation skills I used extensively later in my career.

As one could imagine, with things going so well, I was thinking about ways we could look to expand the business in the LTC pharmacy market in Ohio. I approached Mr. Beeber late in the year about the possibility of opening a new location in Columbus, Ohio, which would provide a way for us to serve more facilities in the Columbus market, as well as reach further into Northeastern Ohio so we could work with a number of nursing facilities there. While he wasn't put off by the suggestion, he was not his usual energetic self about the new opportunity. He said, "Jeff, let's think about a way to expand, however right now we have a growing business here, and the business in Dallas continues to grow very quickly." Again, he was gently warning me, I assumed, not to get the cart ahead of the horse, or, more practically, the ideas ahead of the cash flow! Nonetheless, I took him at his word and mentally tabled the idea to be brought up at a later date.

Not too long after we had this conversation, Mr. Beeber approached me about an inquiry he received from a company in California about buying our operations. I remember part of me being surprised that he would consider such an offer, and another part appreciating what he must have been feeling after having worked so hard for so many years. Maybe it was time for him to "slow down a bit and smell the roses," and perhaps in his mind this was the only way he could envision himself doing just that.

My suspicions were confirmed only a few days later when he approached me one evening as we were about to close the pharmacy. "Jeff," he said. "I have worked many years to develop this business, put in a tremendous number of hours, and made lots of sacrifices both personally and with my family." He continued, "Selling the business to Omnicare, a company with a vision to build a network of LTC pharmacies and create a new business model, makes sense to me. It also allows me to get my money out of the business and do some traveling, which I have always wanted to do." None of what he told me was a surprise, and I was happy for him. I, on the other hand, began thinking about what this would mean for my career given he would no longer be in a position to provide the same support and mentorship, which I had come to appreciate a great deal. Later in the same conversation, he said to me, "Jeff, I would like your help collecting the data Omnicare needs to evaluate the business, as I have not been as involved since you became the operations manager. I am depending on you to organize the information, and to do so in a way that does not create anxiety with the other employees in case the deal does not materialize." I explained to him I understood what he was asking of me, and he could count on me to deliver whatever he needed. It was clear this deal was important to him and because of that, I wanted a positive outcome for him.

Not many days passed before the information requests began coming in about everything from the performance of the business to accounting procedures and the educational background of employees. Virtually every aspect of our pharmacy was being reviewed. Mr. Beeber had explained to me that Omnicare was just beginning to develop its acquisition strategy, and management wanted to ensure there were no missteps, especially early on. (Beeber Pharmacy was the third acquisition Omnicare would attempt in the long-term care pharmacy services marketplace, with the goal of building a large national footprint.)

Mr. Beeber basically let me handle all of the information requests and was gracious enough to let me sit in on some of the strategy meetings to discuss what the deal would look like post-transaction. This was fascinating work, and it was the first time I was exposed to what a company goes through to evaluate a potential business acquisition. While I was busy gathering information, Mr. Beeber investigated the aspects he was most concerned about, such as the price Omnicare would pay for the pharmacy and the structure of the deal.

Several weeks passed in the collection and delivery of the data, and by early 1990, it was clear the deal with Omnicare was headed to a positive conclusion. There were no indications to me we were not going to be acquired by Omnicare. At this point in time, Omnicare was primarily a hospital pharmacy company, and it was declining in profitability because of a new government reimbursement program that created a disincentive for hospitals to outsource their pharmacy services. Beeber Pharmacy was an early target for the new vision of Omnicare, which was to "roll up" (acquire) a fair number of regional pharmacies and then use the volume of those pharmacies to create better buying power and a more consistent product across the entire LTC pharmacy marketplace.

Having worked closely with Mr. Beeber along the way, and knowing Omnicare was aware I was producing much of the requested information, I had some measure of confidence I would have a job with them when the acquisition was completed. I was not sure, however, if I wanted to work for a large company where I might become an "out of sight, out of mind" manager. There were lots of opportunities in the LTC pharmacy market at the time, not only in Ohio (where I had a non-competition agreement with Beeber Pharmacy that I would never have considered violating), but in other states as well. I had started to explore other options not knowing what my future would be with Omnicare. I was soon to find out.

It was about April 1990, and we were fast approaching the closing date for the sale of the pharmacy. Mr. Beeber asked if he could speak with me privately after work. Of course I agreed, and we met after all the other employees had left for the evening. Mr. Beeber began with, "Jeff, I can't thank you enough for all the work you have done to make this deal come together. It has been so rewarding for me to see how you have handled the situation in all aspects." I remember feeling very pleased he was so satisfied with where we were with the potential sale. He continued, "Something has come up, and I need to talk with you about it." I was anxious about what might be next. Were they going to close our pharmacy and move it to the first pharmacy Omnicare had purchased in Cincinnati, resulting in me being out of a job? Was Omnicare dissatisfied with my work on the project in some way? Mr. Beeber continued, "Jeff, Omnicare has approached me and they feel strongly that you must agree to stay for at least one year if they are going to buy the pharmacy. They have seen how involved you are with the operations, the customers, and the staff, and they want you to commit to them for one year!" He never really told me it was a condition of the deal, and I wasn't presumptuous enough to think it was, but I still felt good that the new company wanted me to stay and offered me a raise to boot! All great news!

As we continued to talk in the small pharmacy in Trotwood, Ohio, where Mr. Beeber had undertaken so much innovation in LTC, he offered the following, "Jeff, I think Omnicare will be a great opportunity for you personally. I see them being very successful in their new venture and I think your skills will be appreciated there. Will you give this a try for me?" "Absolutely," was my answer. How could I say no to a man who had invested so much of his time, energy, and money into my development? He also told me that evening, "If you give this a chance, I will make sure you are taken care of." I wasn't exactly sure what he meant by this comment, but by this time I trusted his judgment completely and was confident I would soon find out what he meant. That time was only days away.

May 1, the day of closing with Omnicare, was upon us. I did not go with Mr. Beeber and his business partner to the closing where he was to receive his just reward for all the work he had put in over many years. I was very happy for him as he left for his attorney's office. I was also excited about a new chapter in my career and the careers of the others at Beeber as we prepared to join a new company.

The closing was in the afternoon, and I received a call from Mr. Beeber that all had gone well and the deal had closed. He said to me, "Jeff, Eileen [his wife] and I are going out to celebrate tonight and would like you and your wife to join us at the club. Can you make it?" I told him we would love to and would meet them at his country club. We had a wonderful dinner. Mr. Beeber and I reminisced about all that had happened over the past eight years, and his compliments were very kind and sincere. It was an emotional night in a very positive way. As dinner concluded, Mr. Beeber said to me, "I can't thank you enough for all you did to help get this done. Please accept this as my way of saying thanks in a more tangible way." With that, he slid an envelope across the table, we thanked him for dinner, and left for home. As we drove away, the suspense was too much, so I pulled over to look inside the envelope. In the envelope was a check for five percent of the pharmacy's sale price! I immediately thought of his lesson, "You will never buy anything for yourself that brings you happiness." I imagined that it gave Mr. Beeber great pleasure to be able to do this for me. Sure enough, when I saw him at the pharmacy the next day, he was beaming from ear to ear. Giving my young family a substantial gift and helping me make a promising career move brought him unqualified joy.

CHAPTER 12

Omnicare: The First Year

June 1990 brought many changes to Beeber Pharmacy. First, and most significantly, Omnicare asked Mr. Beeber to assume a more consultative role both with our nursing home customers (as a consultant pharmacist) and throughout the business. After the acquisition, Omnicare asked Mr. Beeber to allow me to manage the business operations, with him assisting me as needed. Given our fairly long history together at this point, Mr. Beeber was not only willing to do this, but was excited about being involved without the heavy burden of ownership on his shoulders. During those first few weeks as we acclimated to our new ownership, more than once Mr. Beeber told us, "This company will be a great opportunity for all of you to grow with this new organization." As always, he remained a constantly encouraging voice during the first several months after the acquisition.

When Mr. Beeber and his partner sold the business to Omnicare, Inc., there was a clause in the contract that only Mr. Beeber, his partner, and I knew about. It was a "hold back clause," which meant that part of the purchase price (and a significant one at that) was withheld during the first year to ensure that the business remained stable. While there was some provision for a modest amount of bed loss (revenue loss), any significant business attrition would dramatically reduce the amount of money Mr. Beeber and his partner would receive from the "hold back" sum that had been set aside. Mr. Beeber and I had discussed this topic prior to the acquisition and he stated several times, "Jeff, we don't lose customers. I am very confident this won't be an issue." While it was not "my pharmacy," I remember having concerns about the unknown, but by this point in our relationship, my trust in Mr. Beeber and his instincts was absolute. Therefore, I put those concerns out of my mind long before the acquisition closed.

Early in the summer of 1990, just a couple short months after the business was sold to Omnicare, the unthinkable happened. Mr. Beeber received a phone call from a very large customer with whom we had enjoyed very positive relationships, not the least of which was Mr. Beeber's friendship with the owner of the company. This owner had been Mr. Beeber's customer since the inception of his business, and they were very strong business partners and friends. The call went as follows: "Bill, I am selling my business to a new company and I wanted to call you to let you know first before you heard it through the grapevine." He stated further, "I am not sure what their intentions are relative to pharmacy, but you know I will do everything I can to keep the contracts with you!" As Mr. Beeber recounted the conversation to me, he was ashen and was clearly concerned because he knew nothing about the company that was acquiring our single largest customer. At the time, this customer represented about 20 percent of our business, and losing them would affect the hold back dollars significantly. I could tell from his reaction he was very worried, however he kept the issue, for the time being, to just his partner, himself, and me.

Within days a second phone call came, this time from the CEO of the new company. He was a young and somewhat brash young man, fairly new to the Ohio market. He conveyed the following message: "We will be transitioning our business to another pharmacy beginning immediately and plan to have the transition completed by early fall. We thank you for your service in the past, however we have a relationship with another pharmacy." To his credit, Mr. Beeber scheduled a meeting with the young CEO, and I attended the meeting to hear what his approach would be. While his presentation was, in my opinion, a very compelling one as to why this was not the best time to move pharmacy services, especially when the company was taking on such a large group of new facilities to manage, the CEO was unwavering in his decision. He ended the meeting with, "Thank you for coming, but we are still moving the business to our current pharmacy partner." I believe this was the first time I ever recall Mr. Beeber appearing panicked. "Jeff," he said, "this will be devastating to me, as you know. I would like you to think about our approach to this problem and how we should address it with Omnicare since you have been working with them for the last few months." I assured him I would do so immediately and began thinking about how we could help Mr. Beeber personally, while at the same time showing Omnicare that we had "courage and forethought" when facing a true challenge. We scheduled a meeting with Omnicare leadership after it was clear the decision of this large customer would not be reversed.

While thinking about several options and discussing each with Mr. Beeber, I felt, and he agreed, we should just be honest. Mr. Beeber finally said, "Jeff, let's just be honest; we will tell them we had no way of knowing this was going to happen, that we apologize, and we will continue to work hard." I remember thinking it sounded a bit passive, but it was the truth. Having dealt only a couple of times with the CEO of Omnicare, Inc., Joel Gemunder, I was not sure how this was going to fly. I suggested to Mr. Beeber that I, rather than he, do the presentation to Joel and the COO. I also suggested that we approach the meeting with Joel by not only explaining the situation described above, but adding the following: "We will replace the beds lost by the end of the year if Omnicare will commit to paying the full amount of the hold back monies should we succeed." It was a bold statement given the competitive nature of the business, however there was nothing to lose and much to be gained. Mr. Beeber would get his money, and the CEO of Omnicare would know he had a good group of managers at Beeber, fully capable of dealing with even the most difficult situations.

The day of the meeting was upon us. Mr. Beeber had agreed to allow me to present our proposal, and the meeting with Joel and the COO went as well as we could have imagined. In fact, at the end of the meeting Joel commented about how impressed he was with our commitment to replace the business in such a short time, however the "proof would be in the results." We left the meeting with Mr. Beeber turning to me and saying, "Great presentation, Jeff. Now what?" He continued, "I hope we can put together a plan to replace the business we have lost." I assured him that I had been working with our group to identify potential customers, and a plan was already forming to begin marketing our services to them immediately. While he was excited about the group's proactive approach, I could tell he was still very worried. I completely understood, as this was his life's work, and not getting paid fully for it seemed terribly unfair to me. While I wanted to make a good impression on my new employer, it was my mentor I really wanted to please. He deserved to get the money he had earned through years of dedicated service and hard work.

Everyone at Beeber worked furiously throughout the remainder of the year and into the early part of 1991. By the one-year anniversary of the sale to Omnicare, the lost business had not only been replaced, but we exceeded the target set during our meeting with Omnicare. Mr. Beeber and his partner received their full purchase price, to the relief of all of us. This story became somewhat legendary with Joel, as he told it many times both as a compliment to me (although it was definitely a group effort) and to encourage those who ran into similar circumstances as Omnicare continued to grow.

Mr. Beeber was not a physically affectionate person with me, but on the day he received the wire transfer for the balance of his purchase price, he gave me a "bear hug" like I had never witnessed him give anyone before. He didn't say "thank you," but I remember the hug being almost a fatherly hug—more "I'm proud of you" than "thank you." It was a special moment between the two of us. I was thrilled that he had received all he deserved for his hard work. It was also at this moment that I remember thinking how the last year had really taken its toll on Mr. Beeber. It seemed as I hugged him that he was way too thin. Given how hard all of us had been working to grow the business while keeping up with our regular customers, I hadn't even noticed he had been losing weight.

CHAPTER 13

Dinner in Dallas

Shortly after Mr. Beeber received his remaining payout, we again started talking about how things were going with AccuCare in Dallas. Cindy was doing an incredible job, and by now the business was really growing and doing extremely well financially. It appeared our cash flow troubles were behind us and the future was looking bright. This business remained a source of pride, as Mr. Beeber would often tell people that he "discovered these two young business people, and look how well they are doing." While flattering to both of us, Cindy was really driving the business. I was simply trying to act as her accountant and doing a modestly successful job of it, to put it mildly.

Early in the summer of 1991, Mr. Beeber wanted me to schedule a trip for him to visit AccuCare, as he had never been "on site" at the business and wanted to see it firsthand. Cindy, of course, was very excited to show off her successful business venture, so she and I scheduled a time in late summer for Mr. Beeber to travel to Dallas to review the business and take a tour. To both Cindy's and my surprise, Mr. Beeber told me, "Jeff, that isn't soon enough, I want to visit as soon as possible." 'Very odd,' I remember thinking, and Cindy and I even spoke about how this was out of character for him. Nonetheless, we scheduled the meeting for just a couple weeks out.

By this time, Mr. Beeber was doing only consultant work at the pharmacy, and I was seeing him less than I had in the many years we had worked together. However when I did see him, he seemed pleased with the lighter load and the ability to spend time doing things he enjoyed without the constant pressure of work. One day he came into the pharmacy after having not been in for a couple of weeks, and I couldn't help but notice his pants were almost falling off him and he was noticeably thinner. Mr. Beeber's natural build was large; he was always in shape for his age, but he was never slender. In today's terminology he would be described as having an "athletic build." His weight loss was becoming quite noticeable, so I inquired about why his weight was going down, and seemingly dramatically. I remember him telling me, "Jeff, I have been on a diet and am finally losing some weight." While he said it with his usual wide grin, something about his explanation of being on a diet did not seem right. Mr. Beeber loved to eat; he was, in fact, a fine diner in every sense of the word and appreciated good food. He had standing nights out on Thursdays and Saturdays and always made sure he took his wife to a nice restaurant or to the club on those evenings. Even with his modest reassurance about being on a diet, I remained concerned that something was amiss with his health. It would not be long before I found out my concern was well placed.

In mid-July 1991, about a week after he had said that dieting was the cause of his weight loss, Mr. Beeber asked me to meet him for lunch on a day when I was working in the pharmacy. During lunch he was somewhat philosophical, talking about my family (by this time my daughter, Sarah, was a little over two years old), things about his family and professional career, and reiterating how pleased he was with how things had turned out with Omnicare. Yet again he said, "Jeff, I really believe this will be a great thing for you that we decided to sell to

Omnicare." He went on to discuss how pleased he was to see Omnicare gaining confidence in my management potential, saying that he could see a time in the near future where they might consider me for additional responsibilities. The conversation was quite out of character for Mr. Beeber, in that he was typically focused on the future, whether it concerned something he was excited about, or something involving others in whom he took an interest. I just knew something was wrong, so I finally just came out with it. "Mr. Beeber, I am concerned about your weight loss. Have you been to a doctor just to make sure something isn't really wrong?" I asked. He looked at me with eyes that looked both tired and sad and said, "Jeff, I have been diagnosed with pancreatic cancer and it has spread to my liver. I probably don't have much longer to live!" I was speechless. This wonderful man, this man who had invested so much in so many—how could this be? It was a very emotional moment for both of us.

He wanted to talk further about the experimental therapies he was trying, seeking to convince himself more than me that they were going to cure his cancer. Being a pharmacist, I knew what it meant when pancreatic cancer had spread to the liver. My mentor would soon be gone. It was a terribly emotional day and, given he didn't want me to tell any of the others, I had to go back to work and keep it to myself. While I was able to do so, immediately upon getting into my car to drive home, the natural emotion of losing someone this important in my life hit me, and the ride home was full of tears and concerns about what his last few months would be like. I didn't want him to be in pain, and this type of cancer is known for causing intense pain. I remember wondering what I could do to help. The trip to Dallas, which he was so excited about, was the first thing that came to my mind. I had to do everything possible to make the trip a great experience for him. I knew he was eagerly anticipating touring the operations of AccuCare, meeting employees, and spending some time with Cindy so he could truly understand how she had grown the business so effectively. I had other plans to take him to some excellent restaurants and was confident this would cheer him up since he loved to eat at nice places.

We left for Dallas and sat together on the plane, where we had more time to talk privately about what he had told me earlier. He spent most of the time talking about family. "Jeff, don't ever let your career make you an absentee father, most especially when your children are young." He reminisced about when his children were younger and how much he worked during those years. I never forgot this advice, and even though I was a busy executive throughout my career, I always kept my commitments to my children. There were specific days (every Wednesday night) when they absolutely knew I would be home early, no matter what. I also attended their games, coached their soccer teams, went to watch the band on Friday nights, and so on. Mr. Beeber's encouragement was instrumental in my seeing the value of investing time and attention in my children.

We arrived in Dallas and Cindy met us at the airport. She and I had arranged for Mr. Beeber to stay at a nice hotel, so we dropped him off and said we would pick him up for dinner. Our tour of the offices would take place the following day. I had told Cindy confidentially about Mr. Beeber's medical condition and how I would like to make this trip fun for him and keep the business matters to the lighter issues.

Cindy and I went to her house so she and I could discuss the next day's activities and include her husband, Joe, in our dinner plans.

Late in the afternoon, Cindy received a call related to AccuCare business, and it was clear she would have to deal with a rather time-consuming matter. She suggested we "guys" take Mr. Beeber out to dinner, so I called him to let him know plans had changed, assuring him we would take him to a very nice restaurant. Mr. Beeber said to me, "Jeff, how about I pick the restaurant? I will let you know where we are going when you get here. Dress casual, as I am not feeling up to a dressy place." I said that would be fine and told Joe about the change.

Joe had never met Mr. Beeber, so he asked about what Mr. Beeber liked and didn't like in restaurants, as well as his favorite types of food and drinks, things he liked to talk about, etc. I made sure he knew Mr. Beeber was not a sports fan of any kind (which both Joe and I were), so we should try to keep the conversation focused on things like points of interest in Dallas and around Texas, local history, business, and our families. I said without hesitation that Mr. Beeber liked fine restaurants, was not a "junk food" eater, rarely drank alcohol, and typically did not stay out very late. Other than sharing these details, I figured we would "play it by ear."

Joe and I left about 5:30 p.m. to pick up Mr. Beeber, and we had some laughs bantering about what restaurant Mr. Beeber might choose and how much it might cost. Within a few minutes we were at the hotel, where Mr. Beeber was outside waiting for us. Mr. Beeber jumped in the back seat, introduced himself to Joe, and said he was excited about a guys' night out. "So where are we going to eat tonight?" I asked. "We're going to a wings joint for some chicken wings and a couple of beers!" The look on Joe's face was priceless, as if to say, "You really know your boss, don't you?" We drove downtown to the restaurant, and when the waitress came over to serve us, Mr. Beeber eagerly belted out, "We will have 50 chicken wings, half mild, half medium, and a pitcher of beer!" I couldn't believe what I was hearing! After the waitress left with our order, Mr. Beeber turned to Joe and asked, "What are the Cowboys' chances of getting to the Super Bowl this year?" Joe and I both chuckled at how wrong I was about Mr. Beeber's dinner and conversation preferences, but I think we both realized he saw this as a chance to forget about being sick for a moment and spend a fun night out with two young men. We spent two hours at the restaurant sharing great conversation, stuffing ourselves with chicken wings, and having a few beers. It was clear Mr. Beeber enjoyed the dinner, and we felt good about showing him a good time.

After dinner, I was expecting him to say he was ready to go back to the hotel, but to my surprise he asked, "What are all those lights across the street? It looks like an arcade." In fact it was an arcade, and he wanted to walk over and take a look. The three of us went inside and played foosball, skeeball, air hockey, and pop-a-shot (a basketball shooting game). Mr. Beeber fared pretty well in all the games against what he called a couple of "in-shape, decent athletes." I could tell he was getting tired, so I suggested we get him back to the hotel and he agreed.

When we dropped him off at the hotel, he shook both our hands and said, "Guys, I can't thank you enough for a great evening. I hope the two of you enjoyed our time together as much as I did." With that he walked into the hotel to retire for the evening. I thanked Joe for being such a good sport, and we laughed out loud over how wrong I was in predicting what the evening would be like.

The next day, we toured the AccuCare operations. Cindy did a great job explaining things to Mr. Beeber, and since she was one of his very favorite people, having her walk him through the operation and introduce him as an owner and investor made him feel very proud. After the tour and a brief meeting, we were off to the airport for the trip home. Mr. Beeber slept almost the entire time on the airplane. It was clear we had worn him out, but what a memory-making trip he had.

Interlude

Shortly after we returned from Dallas, Mr. Beeber's health began to deteriorate rapidly. Over the next few months, Mr. Beeber spent much less time in the pharmacy, and toward the fall, he was not able to come to the pharmacy at all due to his declining health. We did, however, communicate with each other frequently on the phone, and I visited him often to make sure he had the things he needed. Mostly I just wanted to spend some time with him talking about whatever was of interest to him. It was difficult to watch his health deteriorate so quickly, but I realized these would be my last days with my mentor, and I wanted to make sure he knew I was always there for him should he need anything. I, along with others from the pharmacy, assisted Eileen during this difficult time for her. Mr. Beeber entered Hospice of

Dayton late in the year and passed away on January 15, 1992. William Beeber had just had his 65th birthday. My mentor was gone.

To this point, this book has been a chronological account of the nine-year period in which I either worked directly for Mr. Beeber, or we worked together at Beeber Pharmacy after it became part of Omnicare, Inc. As noted, we were also partners in AccuCare Health Services, Inc., for the last two years of Mr. Beeber's life. Some of the lessons that many of us received from Mr. Beeber do not fit chronologically into the story as told to this point. The remaining chapters will describe some of his most consistently delivered lessons and advice. The book will close with some of my observations about how these business/life lessons applied in much larger business venues, and in interpersonal relations overall. Throughout my career, I made it a point to share what I learned from Mr. Beeber, always including a Mr. Beeber story when I was in a position to train others, and always giving him credit where credit was due. As noted in the preface to this book, many in the audience during my training sessions encouraged me to write down the "Mr. Beeber stories." It was those requests that compelled me to write this book in his honor.

Many of the lessons Mr. Beeber imparted were "short and sweet," but what an impact they have if one really puts them into action. Mr. Beeber delivered his advice in a small business environment, however its applicability across businesses of almost every size and complexity has never ceased to amaze me.

CHAPTER 14

Confident, not Cocky

When I first began my career with Mr. Beeber, I was an inexperienced and impressionable young pharmacist. I was confident regarding the clinical aspects of pharmacy, but my self-confidence in dealing with the public and later on with business customers was somewhat low. As I have related, Mr. Beeber was exceedingly generous with his time to help me develop a variety of skills, instilling in me a greater degree of self-assurance with each step of my development. There was, however, one caution that Mr. Beeber discussed with me somewhat regularly: the difference between self-confidence and cockiness.

Anyone who observed Mr. Beeber in action could tell he was a confident man, especially in dealing with customers. I regularly witnessed his self-assured demeanor, however I never saw him come off as cocky or arrogant, either with a customer or an employee. More times than I could count, Mr. Beeber would say to me, "Jeff, self-confidence is a very attractive quality for a manager at any level. Both employees and customers are attracted to this quality." He added, "Customers want to buy their products and services from a confident person, and they will pay a fair price to someone who clearly knows his or her material and products." He acknowledged that some customers would initially do business with the cocky types, but when the opportunity arose, they would gladly switch to someone with a more humble approach. Humility was a word Mr. Beeber used often, typically discussing how "lucky" we were to be involved in a profession that not only helped people but also allowed us to make a good living. "Jeff," he would say, "just remember, whether it is through hard work, luck, or some combination of the two, your life will be much different because you were able to get an education and have a rewarding profession." He often cautioned us about feeling superior because of our education, skills, or talents, because all of us had benefited from good fortune to get where we were. We were privileged to be in a position to help the less fortunate, and we needed to approach everyone with humility and understanding.

When dealing with both customers in the workplace and others in one's personal life, confidence truly is an endearing quality. People gravitate toward it, perhaps because it is so rarely found! Mr. Beeber was willing to be fully involved with everyone in his business, no matter what their position in the company, their education level, or any other factor. Mr. Beeber's quiet confidence, his humility, and his willingness to interact equally with everyone were characteristics that he consistently demonstrated. While he would routinely discuss these attributes with managers in his employ, more importantly, he lived them daily, the results of which we could all witness and learn from.

Later in my career, I was fortunate enough to work into an executive role with Omnicare, which gave me access to countless people at all levels of the organization. I would routinely visit our various pharmacy locations to meet with the regional and local managers, but equally important was the chance to meet with technicians, order entry personnel, billing staff, drivers, and others who daily provided the services we were evaluated on by our customers. It was always my goal to make all those employees feel comfortable with and confident in the company leadership, but more importantly have them be willing to discuss areas where they felt we could improve our operations. Since they were the ones working through the processes every day, who better to provide input and critiques? I always found it quite surprising that many executive managers made decisions about the operations without first truly understanding the business, and moreover without speaking to people in a position to provide valuable input.

As Mr. Beeber said, customers may put up with cockiness if they have no other choice, but when given the chance, they will vote with their feet. Many times I witnessed very talented individuals completely turn off a customer with an overly confident or even aggressive approach. When dealing with customers, I always tried to be confident without seeming brash or pushy. Nonetheless, I'm aware that there were times when I was perceived as being overly self-assured. It happens to everyone who attempts to exude self-confidence, and each time it does, it gives us yet another opportunity to identify what it was about the situation that created negative emotions in the other party. Each encounter presents a growth opportunity to get better. To put it in Mr. Beeber's words, "Confidence sells, cockiness doesn't." Be confident!

CHAPTER 15

The Value of People and Competitive Pay

As I mentioned in Chapter Eight, Mr. Beeber was a man of his word when it came to providing compensation for a job well done. In a broader sense, Mr. Beeber had a philosophy that differs dramatically from the mindset of many in business today. Put simply, he believed that if you find quality people and treat them fairly with competitive pay and a high quality work environment, you will create a stable, professional workforce, which in turn will produce a higher quality product/service.

Each year, Mr. Beeber made sure all his employees were given a written evaluation, and he required every manager to take this process very seriously. When he was responsible for a review, he came up with constructive comments that helped each person develop professionally. I still have some of the reviews given to me by Mr. Beeber. I've kept them as a reminder to spend time with managers under my direction, making sure they received helpful input in as positive a way as possible. At Beeber Pharmacy, the reviews we managers gave employees, as well as the reviews we received, were used in determining the wages all employees would be paid for the following year.

Mr. Beeber believed firmly in paying generously and getting what he considered the "best of the best" in his mind. He never allowed modest amounts of money to stand in the way of increasing the caliber of his staff. He made sure we managers understood that he wanted the best employees in every category and wanted them to be fairly compensated. When I say "fairly compensated," I mean Mr. Beeber's interpretation of that term, which was "more compensation than others who would produce lower quality in the same position at our competition." "Get the best and keep the best," he always said.

Throughout my tenure with Mr. Beeber, especially while managing his business and working with him on business development, losing employees was rare. In fact, I can't recall any dramatic loss of high quality employees. People wanted to work at Beeber Pharmacy, partly because of Mr. Beeber and the management staff he had assembled, but equally, I believe, because he paid a premium wage that allowed us to expect the highest quality of work from employees at all levels.

The stability of the workforce at Beeber Pharmacy was a distinct advantage for those of us who were marketing pharmacy services to potential nursing home clients. We could promise consistent and high quality service, which is something our competitors with much higher employee turnover rates could not provide.

The "competitive pay and value of people" philosophy often brought to our pharmacy the "best of the best" from our competitors. Whenever one of these individuals applied for a position at our pharmacy, Mr. Beeber would say, "Another great employee who understands the business and knows what our customers want, and someone else did all the basic training! Now all we have to do is teach them the Beeber way!"

In today's cut-throat business environment, many executives think nothing of reducing costs by cutting back hourly or lower paid employees. Some business leaders, executives in public companies, and

Wall Street investors view this as an effective approach. It is hardly productive, however, to have employees fearful of losing their jobs. In my opinion, the fear of losing one's job lowers that worker's productivity. In fact, I think resorting to layoffs as a cost-savings measure reflects leaders' inability to grow the business while keeping their own customers totally satisfied. Beeber Pharmacy rarely lost a customer. We retained nearly every customer by having a high-quality, superbly trained, and well-paid staff who made sure the customers were happy. Mr. Beeber didn't have to tell us to keep the customers happy, as we knew our "better than average" livelihood depended on it. On the rare occasion when we would lose a customer, Mr. Beeber never "eliminated staff"; instead, we all went out and found new business. Mr. Beeber's dedication to his employees created the kind of team environment that is rarely seen in today's business world.

Mr. Beeber's philosophy on hiring and keeping good employees still works. While working in my corporate roles over the years, I would occasionally interact with companies that ran their businesses in this manner. Not surprisingly, these businesses were typically very successful. I applaud managers, and especially upper-level executives, who take responsibility for growth so their employees don't have to live in constant fear of losing their jobs. Cost reduction is only a short-term solution to financial stress; a long-term solution requires hir and keeping excellent employees who know how to grow an
a business.

CHAPTER 16

Genuinely Grateful and Sincerely Sorry

While the lesson in Chapter Six about not finding fulfillment in things you buy for yourself was no doubt the most valuable personal lesson Mr. Beeber shared with me, his belief in saying 'thank you' and 'I'm sorry' is without question the most important overall, as it applies to both personal and professional situations.

Mr. Beeber never hesitated to say 'thank you' or 'I'm sorry' whenever it was appropriate to do so. In looking back over the years, I believe the main reasons he was so gracious in this regard were his desire to serve others and his humility. He genuinely wanted others to be satisfied, whether personally or professionally, and he felt bad when they weren't. Likewise, when something went well or he was truly appreciative, he was sure to thank the other person. While I remained his subordinate throughout most of my career, on many occasions he thanked me for something I had done. More importantly, he was man enough to say he was sorry when he was wrong. Watching his genuine use of these terms over my years with him gave me a true appreciation for what being thankful and sorry really meant, and that they weren't terms to be used only in the personal realm. Contrary to what is believed in many circles, they are—or should be—business terms as well.

Mr. Beeber believed that nothing reduces the tension in a negative situation quicker than 'I'm sorry' if it is genuine and appropriate to the situation. While he never used these words as a marketing or sales tool, he thoroughly understood their value in a business setting. Think for a moment about the last business interaction you had with a vendor who was as intent on telling you what you did wrong as on resolving your problem with the service or product. Now, imagine if the vendor had started out the conversation with something like, "I'm very sorry you had a bad experience with our service/product. I will do everything possible to rectify the situation for you. Can we get started on this right away?" What a difference it would make in your reaction! Naturally, people will react less harshly to a negative situation if you first apologize for the problem, especially if it wasn't their fault. Mr. Beeber did this with some regularity, and he had very satisfied customers and employees as a result. This was a lesson I took to heart and used in both personal and business situations throughout my life and business career.

One situation among many comes to mind when I think about how this lesson proved worthwhile. In the fall of 2007 I was asked by the chief operating officer (COO) of Omnicare to manage pharmacy operations in the mid-Atlantic region. In particular, one pharmacy in that region was experiencing serious operational and customer service problems, and those were creating significant patient care issues. Upon being given this assignment, I immediately scheduled a two-day trip to visit this pharmacy so I could evaluate the situation and interact with some very upset customers. I didn't know exactly what I was heading into, but some trusted colleagues let me know the situation was dire, to put it mildly.

One of our best customer's key account manager called me upon hearing that I would be taking over the area and asked me to attend an important meeting as soon as I was scheduled to arrive. While I would have preferred to visit the pharmacy first to get a handle on the issues, I agreed to attend the meeting. Obviously, I had very little time to prepare for this meeting with one of the company's largest accounts (they had multiple LTC facilities in several states). The account manager was very concerned about this meeting because it would include the directors of nursing (DON) from nursing homes across the entire state of Maryland. In addition, the regional DON would be in attendance, as well as the medical director responsible for this area.

The account manager picked me up from the airport and we headed directly to the meeting. She was very nervous and warned me we would be entering the "lions' den," with many of the nurses being very upset with our services. I had asked one of our regional pharmacy operations managers to attend with me to take notes and gain valuable experience in handling dissatisfied customers. Given how nervous our key account manager was, I asked her to make an opening statement, add some general comments, and then I would take over. I told her if she felt uncomfortable with anything that happened, she could just introduce me and I would jump in—in other words, she didn't have to wait if things escalated quickly. She warned me that the COO and my predecessor had attended a similar meeting several months before and had made promises about improving our services, none of which had come to fruition. This turned out to be a critical piece of information.

When we arrived, there was literally standing room only in a very large conference area, with approximately 50 people in the room. The account manager introduced herself and began her opening comments. Immediately one of the nurses stood up and stated, "We don't care about anything other than getting the right drug to the right patient at the right time, and frankly we don't even care if you bill it correctly!" With that, the account manager turned immediately to me and said, "I'd like to introduce our Senior Vice President of Operations, Jeff Stamps." I took the floor and before I could even get past "good morning," the regional DON said, "We have had suits from your company here before and nothing has gotten done. What are you going to do to make a difference?" Wow, I thought, it's a 'lions' den' all right! Rather than making further statements, I simply opened the floor for comments from what was clearly a very disgruntled group of nurses, and comment they did. I listened for about 45 minutes to a host of issues being brought up by the nurses. Thankfully, our regional operations manager was dutifully writing them all down so we could have a complete list of their complaints to guide our development of a plan to correct the issues raised at the meeting.

When the comments were getting less "angry" in nature, I said the following: "I'm very sorry you have had and continue to have serious issues with our services, and I feel terrible about the additional burden this is placing on you as caregivers for your residents." You could feel the tension dissipate almost immediately. I continued, "I don't have the answers to your concerns today, but I commit to you when I leave this meeting I will immediately travel to the pharmacy and begin the work to improve our services. I ask that you give me ninety days, and I promise you will see a difference." I realized it was risky asking for a second chance since my predecessor had done very little to solve the problems, but they agreed. The regional nursing director stated, "We expect you to attend our next meeting in ninety days. I suggest you make something happen." My team and I left the meeting and proceeded to the pharmacy, where we immediately began reviewing the areas related to their most significant issues. Over the next several months, we brought in a team of our best operations support personnel and overhauled the pharmacy virtually top to bottom, including relieving the general manager of his duties.

The team did a fantastic job turning the operations around, and I returned to the nurses' next quarterly meeting with my key account manager and regional operations manager ninety days later. As I stood up to address the same people who had frankly been interested in throwing us out three months before, they gave us a standing ovation! Additionally, the regional nursing director, who had been very aggressive in the first meeting, stated, "I had no confidence you could make a difference, but you clearly have and we are very appreciative. Now you have to make sure it remains at this level." While the compliment was directed at me, it was clearly the effort of a talented team that turned the situation around. I believe strongly that had I not genuinely apologized for a poor level of service, but rather tried to justify what we were doing or worse yet, do as my predecessor had done and imply the nurses at the facilities were somehow at fault, this account would have been at significant risk of being lost. In the years after this episode, the key account manager and I told this story many times, and we laughed about it often while I was with the company.

Another positive outcome from that terrible situation was my opportunity to meet with the COO of this customer a few weeks later. He thanked me for my team's efforts to "right the ship," which in turn took the pressure off him related to the poor service his nurses had been complaining about. This COO and I continued to maintain a positive peer-to-peer relationship throughout my tenure at Omnicare.

'I'm sorry' can also be a valuable tool when working with employees whom you supervise. When the boss has the humility to apologize for doing something wrong, it lets the employees know the boss is human and is willing to admit he or she could have handled a matter more effectively. Furthermore, it builds trust because employees see they will not be blamed for something that wasn't their fault. This part of leadership can be difficult, but without it, in my opinion, your staff will never truly trust or respect you as a leader.

Mr. Beeber often thanked me for efforts related to the business. While it wasn't something I felt he needed to do (I knew when something had been done well), it always made me feel as though he recognized and appreciated a good effort. As the years went by, he thanked me less, possibly because he knew I didn't have the type of personality that needed it, but he never stopped saying thank you when appropriate. Whether used in a professional setting or in one's personal life, 'thank you' and 'I'm sorry' are invaluable phrases when used sincerely.

CHAPTER 17

Quality – Service – Price

Quality, service, and price are three aspects of virtually everything consumed in our market economy, whether applied to a car, groceries, Internet and television services, or any other consumable product. I remember Mr. Beeber teaching me about this concept on my very first day of work. He believed strongly these three components were factors in every buying decision. Awareness of these three elements played an integral role in the development of his, and subsequently my, approach to selling pharmacy services.

Mr. Beeber's basic premise was as follows: these three factors can each be manipulated to some degree to create an overall value proposition in the mind of the consumer; in our case the consumer was the nursing home decision maker relative to pharmacy services. While he felt you could tweak all of the components, it was virtually impossible to be the best in all three categories for a given good or service. For instance, if you wanted to deliver the best quality and the best service, you could not do so at the lowest price. From another perspective, if you were aiming to offer the lowest price for a service/product, some aspect of quality or service would have to be sacrificed. While this concept is not universally accepted, I happen to agree with his premise and used it as a foundation of marketing presentations I made for the duration of my career.

To look at this in a more simplistic way, let's look at purchasing an automobile. If you plan to purchase a car, you are faced with a wide array of choices. If you want the luxury and performance of a Cadillac Escalade and the service associated with a vehicle of this nature, you will not be able to purchase it at the price of a vehicle of lower quality. The cost of building the Cadillac is higher (due to its more sophisticated features), so those who choose to purchase it value quality (and service) above price. This is a simple example, but it can be applied to a more complex business model such as long-term care pharmacy services. One could argue that since patient health and well-being are in play in the nursing home setting, quality and service become even more critical considerations than they would with a consumer product.

I recall the first time I heard Mr. Beeber explain this concept eloquently to a potential customer. During the presentation, he discussed the product (which in this case was the actual medications to be provided), the distribution procedures, and the accounting and medical record systems in place to assist nurses in administering medications to residents of the long-term care facility. Although the only tangible product being purchased by the customer was medication, the quality and service aspects associated with the distribution system were equally, if not more, important to the nurses who administered medications and had to document their use. Beeber Pharmacy was well known for having the highest quality medical record programs, however this excellence came at a price for the customer. Mr. Beeber wisely addressed how customers could get the medications at a "cheaper" price, but in so choosing they would be making sacrifices in the quality of the record keeping system and in the level of service the facility could expect from a provider other than Beeber Pharmacy.

In the early days of the long-term care pharmacy specialty (late 1970s and early 1980s) the technology and service levels were very unsophisticated compared to today's standards, and there were significant differences from one competitor to another. Mr. Beeber was very effective at explaining why we charged a slight premium over our competitors. The customers who chose us clearly understood the value of having higher quality and better service instead of focusing only on the price of the medications. Said differently, the higher quality and better service we offered resulted in a lower "cost" when one considered how quality and service impacted the overall operating costs of the nursing home. Our challenge boiled down to creating an understanding that there was a significant difference between the "price of the medications" and the "cost" of the service. This concept has proven itself to be true in today's long-term care market, as well as in many other service and product businesses.

After Beeber Pharmacy was purchased by Omnicare, Inc., the business continued to grow in complexity, as patients with higher and higher acuity levels were being admitted to nursing homes. Additionally, more and more services were developed to increase the accuracy and ease of dispensing medications in order to reduce the workload of the nursing staff. From 1993 until my retirement in November of 2012, these developments continued at a rapid pace, however the critical interaction of quality, service, and price never changed.

Throughout my career, I was privileged to be in a position to negotiate many contracts, some in the thousands of dollars and some in the hundreds of millions. Being a first-hand observer of Mr. Beeber's marketing techniques allowed me to build on his paradigm of quality, service, and price as I interacted with nursing home administrators, COOs, and CEOs of very large companies across America. I appreciated having this foundational principle to carry with me throughout my career, and each time I discussed it, I thought about Mr. Beeber letting me sit in the chair beside him while he presented on the topic. It was truly an invaluable lesson passed along by my mentor.

In addition to negotiating contracts using this concept, I employed it in countless training sessions with the sales staff. I can't recall a single training session where I did not speak at length about these three aspects of the selling process. Once our salespeople understood the difference between the "price of the medications" and the "cost" of the overall service to the customer, I believe they became more effective. During these training sessions I always credited Mr. Beeber for his insights and am quite confident, based on the comments I routinely received, that the salespeople found great worth in the explanation. It was always heartwarming for me to think that Mr. Beeber's lessons continued to hold value years after his passing, even though many aspects of the LTC pharmacy environment had changed so dramatically. Those who really understood the difference between price and cost became better operators, better salespeople, and better consumers of services, ultimately resulting in higher quality patient care in LTC nursing facilities.

CHAPTER 18

"Never let a 'superstar' leave your company"

As I previously mentioned, Mr. Beeber valued his employees and was willing to pay a premium to attract good talent. He believed strongly in never letting a truly talented person leave his business, unless of course there were personal reasons for doing so such as a family move, health issues, retirement, etc. That said, I found that as I progressed in a larger company, this approach didn't always work as well as it did in a "family" business. For instance, I believe as mentors and developers of young managers, we owe it to them to help them move on if it is clear their career path in the current company will not allow them to realize their full professional and financial potential. Throughout my executive career, some excellent managers went elsewhere because they felt there were not suitable opportunities for upward mobility (a reasonable expectation to be promoted and subsequently improve their income level). In those cases, I rarely tried to talk them out of it, because I realized doing so would just reduce their satisfaction with their current position, create less trust in me, and ultimately result in them leaving the company under negative circumstances. Frankly, when they moved on to positions that brought them increased success, even when they ultimately became competitors, I still felt we had done the right thing by not trying to convince them to stay. Nonetheless, there are some circumstances when it clearly makes sense to keep a superstar, and that is absolutely the case in some smaller business situations.

This lesson came about through a situation at Beeber Pharmacy before it was purchased by Omnicare, Inc. As previously mentioned, Gina Pruitt (Timmons) came to work with us after she graduated from pharmacy school. Gina was an excellent pharmacist who was very accurate and had a great understanding of customer service as well. Her outstanding communication skills, computer expertise, clinical acumen, and pleasant approach with customers made her a valuable asset to the business very quickly. Since Gina had aspirations to further her career, she looked for and was offered a position by a retail pharmacy that would pay her a higher salary, enabling her to further her education. She informed me of her intent to resign, and I was disappointed to say the least. I knew I needed to let Mr. Beeber know she would be leaving the company.

I approached Mr. Beeber late one evening to tell him the news. While we all thought very highly of Gina as our colleague, there was no one in the pharmacy who appreciated Gina's skill and enthusiasm more than Mr. Beeber did. I can still recall the look of disappointment on his face when I told him Gina would be moving to another company for more money. Not surprisingly, after a moment's thought, he stated almost defiantly, "Jeff, Gina Pruitt is a superstar. You don't let superstars leave your company over money if the salary of the other position is within reason and that is truly the reason for leaving." I was confident Gina was only leaving for the additional salary, because she had told me so herself. I knew she enjoyed her job and the people she worked with, and she appreciated the knowledge she was gaining at Beeber Pharmacy. I relayed all this to Mr. Beeber, and he replied, "Jeff, pay her the salary she needs in order to stay. Gina will find a way to make up the additional salary and then some; I am confident of this." I had my marching orders, and I remember hoping the conversation with Gina would go well and that she would decide to stay.

The next day I informed Gina of the discussion I had with Mr. Beeber and asked if she would be willing to stay for a higher salary. Thankfully, she agreed to stay with Beeber Pharmacy. As mentioned earlier, Gina is now a leader in the LTC pharmacy industry, having become an expert in helping facilities provide better care for their residents through the appropriate use of pharmacy data.

Mr. Beeber was thrilled with Gina's decision to stay in his employ, and I remember the big Beeber bear hug he gave Gina when he learned she would not be leaving. Although in my career, as referenced above, I sometimes let a top performer move on if it was in his or her best interest to do so, I have always valued Mr. Beeber's commitment to hiring and keeping "superstars" whenever possible.

CHAPTER 19

Be an Expert

As has been explained many times in this book, Mr. Beeber believed strongly that a pharmacist must thoroughly understand the entire business in order to be successful. In the LTC pharmacy field, a pharmacist must know about drug distribution and packaging systems, medical record systems, special purchasing requirements, narcotic regulations (procuring and destroying as necessary), clinical operations, and customer service, to name just a few aspects. Mr. Beeber believed you could only obtain the necessary knowledge about the different aspects through direct, hands-on, experience. I have previously described how Mr. Beeber expected me to learn about every facet of the LTC pharmacy business. While I was interested in some, but not all, of these areas, he nonetheless required me to become an expert in all of them. What set Mr. Beeber apart in his training techniques, however, was his insistence that his pharmacists know their customers' business just as well. He wanted us to understand how our products and services fit into the business model of each customer. Mr. Beeber was very clear that becoming an expert at your customer's business, as well as your own, was a much different concept than being an expert at only how your business functioned.

Early on, when I was more interested in the clinical side of the business, and after Mr. Beeber finally allowed me to be a consultant pharmacist, I was exposed to all the internal workings of a nursing home, not just the pharmacy function. As the clinical pharmacist for a facility, I was involved in meetings with the director of nursing, the medical director, physical and occupational therapists, dieticians, and other ancillary professionals (podiatrists, dentists, optometrists, and dieticians). Most importantly, I interacted with the staff nurses and nursing assistants who used our products and services on a daily basis. If there were problems related to pharmacy, you could rest assured the staff nurses and nursing assistants were fully aware of them and were more than willing to give you an earful if they were only asked. I was blessed to work in facilities with some of the most knowledgeable and conscientious nurses, physicians, and administrators around. During those formative years, many of these professionals took their time to explain their business to me, in depth and without reservation, allowing me to become educated about the business more quickly than if I had not had those interactions.

When it came time to sell Beeber Pharmacy to Omnicare, Mr. Beeber was quite proud that his "hand-picked" group of pharmacists had become experts in LTC pharmacy because he had trained us to learn both our own business and the customers' business. He was confident that we were well trained and could help the new company grow in the future. One day shortly before Omnicare acquired us, he pulled me aside and said, "Jeff, because of your experiences with Beeber Pharmacy to this point, you are well prepared to move into roles with greater responsibility with this new company. I believe Omnicare will be a great opportunity for you to expand on what you have learned here. How exciting to be able to use those skills to help shape this new company!" While he didn't say it outright, I think he meant, "Jeff, I have taught you what I can teach you and now you will have your chance to put your own personal touches on those lessons, most likely on a bigger stage."

Beeber Pharmacy was Omnicare's third acquisition, and the growth the company experienced over the next several years was phenomenal to say the least. Because of my experiences at Beeber Pharmacy, and the expertise I was able to develop under Mr. Beeber's guidance, several career opportunities presented themselves, each with increasing responsibility. I never lost sight of Mr. Beeber's requirement to "be an expert." My training put me in a unique position to help correct operational issues in the pharmacies Omnicare acquired. My mentor prepared me well for the challenges I faced in my career.

In the later years in my career, what an advantage it was to have the full understanding of the industry afforded me through Mr. Beeber. Because I gained so much hands-on experience at Beeber, I was better equipped to solve operational problems, address issues in clients' facilities, and negotiate contracts in a way that was fair to the customer but profitable for the company. Without the expectation to "be an expert," there would have been many times I would have been at a disadvantage during contract negotiations. I needed to convince customers that they were dealing with an individual who thoroughly understood their business, even if they were not successful at getting everything they wanted at the negotiating table.

In total, I spent nine years working side by side with Mr. Beeber. He was an incredibly hard worker, instilling a sense of urgency throughout the pharmacy, and always pushing for prompt, high-quality services. For the first few years I worked with him, I observed his work ethic, whether he was in the pharmacy, in a client nursing facility, or in the community trying to attract new clients. He reminded me regularly how important it was to understand the "grunt" aspects of the LTC pharmacy business. I used the term "grunt pharmacist" many times throughout my career, with great respect for Mr. Beeber as I did. While some found this designation to be demeaning and not worthy of an executive in the largest LTC pharmacy company in the United States, I typically used it to reinforce to those under my direction how important it was to understand the "grunt" or detailed aspects of our business. In addition, I mentioned it on occasion with customers and potential customers to convey, in a somewhat subtle and humble way, that I was an expert in this business and knew the basics of the business along with the more sophisticated aspects of contract negotiation.

I have heard people describe Mr. Beeber as "homespun," not in a demeaning way, but as a term of respect. There were those throughout my career who commented that this same "homespun" style in me would impede my upward mobility in the LTC pharmacy business. I was told I needed to have a more executive presence. Frankly, I never had much respect for those who held this opinion. Typically, such comments came from executives who had long lost the ability to relate with customers, and never from a person I considered to be a true leader.

Executives have lots of different styles and many of them can be effective. The "homespun" style worked well for me throughout my career. Mr. Beeber imparted to me the basics of this style, and I believe he would have felt I improved upon the lessons he taught me by becoming an executive who produced results, created confidence in customers, and was approachable and flexible with employees. Anyone who knew Mr. Beeber would be honored to model himself or herself after Mr. Beeber's masterful example.

112

CHAPTER 20

Cultivating Relationships

Mr. Beeber was a relationship builder, something I recognized as far back as my first day of my employment in 1982. As we were gathering information at the nursing facility that day, I dutifully copied various documents and recorded data from several sources, while Mr. Beeber took the time to introduce himself to every single nurse he encountered. At the time, I just thought he was being friendly, but as I worked with him more and more, I realized he was building as many positive relationships as he could. He established relationships at every level of his business, including with the owners, administrators, directors of nursing, staff nurses, and sometimes even with lenders associated with our clients. He also built solid relationships with his employees, which in the LTC pharmacy industry means everyone from people with advanced degrees to some who had not finished high school.

Mr. Beeber viewed interpersonal relationships as being critical in a business where perfection in service delivery was simply not attainable. No matter how hard we tried to provide excellent service, problems inevitably arose that needed to be worked out with our clients. On numerous occasions, Mr. Beeber would say to me, "Jeff, if you are nothing more than a vendor, you will rarely get a second chance should something go wrong with your service, even if it is a small thing." He continued, "However, if you have a genuine relationship with your customers, it will earn you a second chance

113

should you experience problems or concerns about your service in a facility." At first I really did not grasp the importance of this lesson, but as I worked those many years in the LTC pharmacy industry, it became abundantly clear to me how important this lesson really was.

Not only did I spend a significant amount of time on the development of positive relationships within the business I was responsible for, I encouraged those who worked in my organization to do the same. As mentioned earlier in the book, I was routinely involved in the training of sales and operations executives, and in every single presentation, I reinforced the importance of cultivating positive relationships. While it's true that getting a second chance still means you must perform well to keep the business, at least you stay "in the game" versus simply being terminated outright. Later in my career, when the number of clients was in the thousands (versus fewer than one hundred that we had at Beeber Pharmacy), it was essential that a focus on relationships be embraced throughout the organization. I was fortunate in that almost all of the professionals with whom I worked believed in this concept, and as a result we were very strong in this dimension. Although we did lose customers occasionally, we improved our customer retention rate by almost five percent during the last two years of my career when this became a company-wide focus.

Some people don't subscribe to this relationship-based view of customer relations, as they believe their job is to connect with a company, not with the individual employees in it. I don't embrace this view, because I have seen how essential it is to build interpersonal trust so if you need a second chance, the people who have come to know and trust you will be inclined to give you that chance.

I mentioned earlier a meeting I had in Maryland with a very large customer, and how our team successfully corrected problems that the customer was having with our service. During that same visit to Maryland, I was contacted by a customer I met when marketing our services. In the course of making several presentations to this customer, I had developed a positive relationship with the CEO, as he and I had much in common (we are both big sports fans and love to play golf). Recalling Mr. Beeber's lesson about relationship building, I decided to reach out to this CEO to ask how things were going. Given what I had heard at the volatile meeting described in Chapter 16, I fully expected to hear some nightmarish comments about our service. When I called him, he said, "Jeff, thank you for calling me. I really need your help. My nurses are all over me about pharmacy problems. I know you are just taking over this region, but I have to tell you I can't hold off my staff much longer. If you can't get the service levels where they need to be to satisfy my nurses, I will have to move the business elsewhere." I knew from the other customer meeting that this was an emergency, but I also felt I had built up enough credibility to get a chance to "fix" his company's issues and maintain the business.

The team we assembled to work on the operations of this pharmacy did a remarkable job, and we reached a satisfactory outcome with this customer just as we did with the large customer mentioned earlier. The relationship I developed with this CEO continued throughout the last several years of my career with Omnicare, and remained a positive one until my retirement.

While Mr. Beeber never provided me with a roadmap of how to build relationships with customers, two of the tools I used were personal phone calls and handwritten notes. I routinely called customers just to inquire about their satisfaction level with our company. The input I received was always valuable in making improvements in how we did business. I made the handwritten notes personal, typically mentioning something positive about the customer's business or an important event in his or her life. I believe these notes conveyed that the relationship was worth my time and that I cared about that person and the company. In today's business environment, which is characterized by automation and impersonal call centers, developing and maintaining business relationships still matters.

CHAPTER 21

Thoughts from a Thirty-Year Career

In today's business environment, spending thirty years in one industry is quite unique. Since retiring from my position in November 2012, some people have told me that staying in the same industry so long was a mistake. I understand the reasons they hold this view, however I have always felt the LTC pharmacy industry exposed me to virtually every aspect of business and gave me transferable skills that apply no matter what service or product is being sold.

As this book has made clear, everything about my career would have been different were it not for Mr. Beeber. Friends and colleagues over the years have commented how lucky I was to walk into that pharmacy in a strip mall in Trotwood, Ohio, and ask for a job. Was I lucky to meet Mr. Beeber and receive the business and life lessons I have memorialized in this book? Of course. Luck, or good fortune, if you prefer to call it that, is part of every successful professional's career whether a person acknowledges it or not. It might come in the form of meeting a key mentor, having a big account fall in your lap, being treated poorly in a way that motivates you to succeed, or landing a promotion because the person ahead of you left the company. Some people capitalize on these twists and turns in a business career and some don't. I have always found it interesting to hear the supremely self-confident business people I've known over the years tell how they became successful on their own. I think it says something about a person if he or she does not recognize how a mentor, a lucky break, or the good work of others contributed to his or her accomplishments. The most respected leaders I rubbed shoulders with never claimed to be "self-made," and they were more than willing to credit other people and circumstances for the success they came to enjoy.

Businesses come in all sizes and shapes, and clearly with the boom in technology, the landscape of business is ever changing. Nonetheless, some of the simplest principles are the best ones. As Mr. Beeber taught me and as I learned from my own experience, cultivating positive personal relationships in business is paramount. In this day and age, there are a myriad of electronic ways to communicate with customers and business associates, whether through Twitter, Facebook, e-mail, or texting. While these methods are convenient and afford a rapid exchange of information, they should never replace face-to-face contact or other means of conversation (telephone, videoconferencing, etc.). It takes time to get to know customers and become intimately familiar with their business needs, but the payoff comes in having satisfied and loyal customers who speak well of your company to others and will stick with you when problems arise. In addition, it is a rewarding and fulfilling way for you to do business as you make personal, and sometimes lifelong, connections with people in your industry. And from a purely practical standpoint, developing personal relationships with your customers gives you a leg up on your competitors!

Another simple but invaluable principle is the importance of thanking customers for their business. Since there is no shortage of competitors that they could choose to do business with, saying "thank you" is essential in building loyalty and positive regard. A "thank you" message can be delivered in a host of ways: through personal meetings, correspondence, call center interactions, and even on web pages. Never leave your customers wondering whether you value their business. The same applies for potential customers: thank them for considering doing business with you, and leave no doubt that they would be well served by your company.

On top of everything else Mr. Beeber taught me as my mentor, he showed me what it takes to be a good mentor. I have often been asked why Mr. Beeber was willing to invest so much time and attention in me. I don't know the answer to that, but I will be forever grateful that he enriched my personal and professional life by teaching me so much.

The nature of the mentoring relationship is such that the mentor always knows more than the person he/she is mentoring when the process begins. The mentor's responsibility, in my mind, is to pass along everything he or she possibly can in hopes that the person being mentored will expand on that knowledge and make the business process or product better. Inevitably the person being mentored, if the mentor has selected a person with good potential, will become "smarter" than the boss in at least a few areas of the business. Did I know more about certain aspects of the business than Mr. Beeber? No question, as it was my job to attend to things he didn't have time to keep track of and thus delegated to me. In order to get the full benefit from your mentor, you must be humble enough to know that while you may acquire more expertise than your mentor in certain areas, you still have a lot to learn. The training process can take years, and the person being mentored has the responsibility (yes, I mean responsibility) to apply the lessons that are taught and to build on them to make the business even better. If done right, mentoring never stops, because just as you received guidance and instruction from your mentor, you owe it to the next generation of leaders to invest in someone else. Unfortunately Mr. Beeber did not live long enough to witness how his lessons came to fruition in those he trained, but I believe he would be glad that we made good use of what he taught us. If you are blessed to have a mentor—someone who takes a special interest in your personal and professional development—have the humility to learn all you can, build on it, invest in someone else, and never forget the person who poured himself or herself into your life.

One indicator of the impact Mr. Beeber made on many in his industry is the golf tournament that was held in his honor for 20 years. A couple of years after his death, a group of his former associates started the William Beeber Memorial Golf Tournament for the purpose of raising scholarship money for pharmacy students. The tournament chairman of this event was Rick Bachman, a pharmacist who came to work for Beeber Pharmacy before its acquisition by Omnicare and someone who also benefited from Mr. Beeber's kindness. I want to thank Rick, and those who helped him each year, for their dedication to this cause and for keeping Mr. Beeber's memory alive through the students being supported. During the 20 years the tournament was held, not a single tournament date was rained out. We like to think Mr. Beeber played a hand in arranging such beautiful weather so the tournament (and fundraising) could go on as planned. In twenty years, more than $150,000 was raised to assist the "Beeber Scholars," as we affectionately called them. The tournament represents yet another way

Mr. Beeber invested in the next generation of pharmacists and supported a profession that he loved.

I hope I have conveyed some of the ways William Beeber impacted my life and the life of many others. By and large, his lessons were simple but time-tested: be prompt, work hard, look the part of a professional, give credit where it is due, be humble, find joy in giving to others, say 'thank you' and 'I'm sorry' when appropriate, be true to your word, be confident (not cocky), value the work of good employees, cultivate relationships, and strive to be an expert in all aspects of your business. All of these lessons have been relevant and applicable in both my career and my personal life. As if these weren't enough, he also taught me the single most useful principle that has guided my professional career: always remember the critical interrelationship of quality, service, and price!

It is rare in life to encounter a person so influential and so committed to generously sharing his or her knowledge and life experience for the betterment of others. Knowing Mr. Beeber—whether it came about through serendipity, luck, or fate—has been one of the great blessings of my life. I will always be grateful for his investment in me that enabled me to have a rewarding and fulfilling career in a profession we both loved. It has been my goal to impact others in the same positive way that he influenced me. So thank you, Mr. Beeber, for sharing your life and your wisdom with many. I, for one, can say "it mattered to me!"

Acknowledgments

I thank my wife, Nancy, for listening to my Mr. Beeber stories over the many years we've been together, and for encouraging me to complete this book in his honor.

I offer special thanks to my editor, Susan Bradley, who meticulously sharpened my sentences as I wrote them, corrected my punctuation mistakes, taught me the appropriate use of "which and that," and most importantly, kept me focused on creating a book to honor Mr. Beeber and nothing more.

Last, but certainly not least, I thank my parents, Boyd and Olive Stamps, whose hard work, encouragement, and financial backing created the opportunity for me to become a pharmacist. Without their support, I would never have met Mr. Beeber, and my life would most certainly have taken a different course.

CPSIA information can be obtained at www.ICGtesting.com
Printed in the USA
LVOW01s2018090714

393592LV00026B/808/P

9 781495 316173